The Qur'anic Narrative

The Qur'anic Narrative
The Journey of Life as Told in the Qur'an

LOUAY M. SAFI

Westport, Connecticut
London

Library of Congress Cataloging-in-Publication Data

Safi, Lu'ayy.
    The Qur'anic narrative : the journey of life as told in the Qur'an / Louay M. Safi.
        p. cm.
    Includes bibliographical references and index.
    ISBN 978–0–313–36199–9 (alk. paper)
1. Life in the Koran. 2. Koran—Theology. 3. Religious life—Islam. 4. Koran—Criticism,
interpretation, etc. I. Title.
BP134.L54S24   2008
297.1'226—dc22   2008023721

British Library Cataloguing in Publication Data is available.

Library of Congress Catalog Card Number: 2008023721
ISBN: 978–0–313–36199–9

First published in 2008

Praeger Publishers, 88 Post Road West, Westport, CT 06881
An imprint of Greenwood Publishing Group, Inc.
www.praeger.com

Printed in the United States of America

The paper used in this book complies with the
Permanent Paper Standard issued by the National
Information Standards Organization (Z39.48–1984).

10 9 8 7 6 5 4 3 2 1

Contents

Preface

The observable world manifests its intricate diversity in a vast space that endlessly expands through time. The colorful shades and beautiful contours of that space are observed with the light of brilliant stars. The sun rises every day to reveal the beauty of imposing mountains, vast seas, and open skies. Through the rays of light that shine we are able to observe the beauty of the creation and delight our eyes with every color and shape.

Behind the observable world, and beyond the reach of human senses, lies a world of greater beauty and brilliance, with the power to move us intellectually and emotionally in more diverse and more profound ways. The world of spirit, though hidden and concealed, is the essence of the observable world. Without an intelligent spirit to conceive and contemplate and a passionate spirit to desire and appreciate, the observable world would have never been, because it would have never been contemplated or comprehended. The world and the word are, therefore, forever intertwined.

The revealed word has always inspired people to rise above their immediate experiences, to reach out to a higher ground and contemplate new horizons and possibilities. With the power of hope and the strength of relentless faith, humanity grew and evolved in knowledge and tools. Yet religion that often motivated and inspired people to reach to the stars has repeatedly degenerated into a blind zeal, sending the zealots crashing down on their fellow travelers through the journey of life.

Islam, like all divine revelations, has over the centuries produced sublime spirits, whose energies and contributions have made life a better place, as it has produced zealots bent on turning the revealed message over on its head. The Qur'an, the foundational document of the Islamic faith, has been read as an inspirational message of hope, compassion, duty, and fairness, as it has been read as a template for intolerance, hate, imposition, and revenge. This book stresses that a fair, balanced, and engaging reading of the Qur'an is bound to produce a message of peace, compassion, and hope.

The Qur'anic Narrative attempts to capture the essence of the Qur'anic message. It does that by identifying key Qur'anic concepts and themes and weaving them into a wholesome narrative that uncovers the essence of the Qur'anic message. *The Qur'anic Narrative* aspires to show that the Qur'an has an inspiring message, whose aim is to enlighten the path of those who wholeheartedly embrace it and to guide them through the journey of life.

ACKNOWLEDGMENTS

In writing this book, I have been inspired and supported by countless people. To acknowledge their contributions in this limited space is virtually impossible. I can only say that in my quest for meaning and purpose, I am indebted to the thoughts, words, and actions of teachers, students, friends, and companions of my life journey. I am forever grateful to all of them for their example, encouragement, trust, and support.

I must single out, though, a few individuals whose support has been essential for writing and publishing this book.

I would like to thank several friends and scholars who agreed to read the manuscript and provide me their feedback and comments. Seyyed Hossein Nasr, Aminah McCloud, Sulayman Nyang, Ingrid Mattson, Charles Butterworth, and Scott Alexander have read the manuscript, in part or in whole, and shared with me their fine comments and thoughts, and I am grateful to them all. I would like also to express my deep appreciation to Suzanne Staszak-Silva and Elizabeth Claeys for their superb professionalism and editorial support, and for making the experience of publishing this book pleasant.

I am indebted to my mother Hana, for her big and caring heart and for teaching me the meaning of resilience, patience, sacrifice, and unconditional love.

I am grateful to my wife Razan, for her loving heart and helping hands. Her unfailing support and encouragement have allowed me to devote considerable time to intellectual pursuits and public service.

I am also grateful for the inspiration I have always received from our four children, who have been the joy of our lives—Lubna, Rahaf, Munir, and Mackeen. I hope this book will inspire them and provide them, along with other young spirits, with fresh reflections as they embark on the journey of life. Their loving and generous hearts have made my life's journey easier to travel.

My profoundest gratitude is reserved to the source of all joy, inspiration, knowledge, and gratitude, whose Compassionate Spirit has immensely blessed humanity and made life worth living.

Introduction

The Qur'anic Narrative purports to recapture the Islamic spirit promoted in the Qur'an, which historically gave rise to a towering civilization that permeated much of the world for over a millennium, whose achievements form the foundation of modern society. It tries to paste together a narrative that is both consistent and representative of the overall Qur'anic message. The narrative that emerges in the various chapters of the book is outlined by undertaking a thematic reading of the Qur'an. The book identifies the major themes that dominate the Qur'anic passages. The message that emerges is one of peace and hope.

Given the close relation between the method of reading the Qur'anic text and the interpretation that results from that reading, we must begin by examining the relationship between meaning and method and by asking the crucial questions that reveal this relationship: how does one read a revealed book whose first recipients lived in a time and place of particular social and historical conditions? How does one understand the intended meaning of the revealed text in ways that do not confuse it with historical experiences and interpretations? And how does one relate the intended meaning to an evolving human condition?

Understanding the revealed text is both a simple task and a complex enterprise. It is a simple task for those who constantly return to the text desiring wisdom and understanding and seeking religious inspiration and moral guidance. The task is markedly more complex for those who want to provide a systematic presentation of the divine message. For here one is faced with another layer of difficulty, as one encounters in this case a set of parallel texts, developed by scholars and intellectuals, that are used to interpret and explain the original text. The interpretations are often colored by the spirit of the times in which they have taken place.

The interpretations are often influenced by the social, political, and educational conditions of the early societies.

The Qur'anic Narrative aims to capture the intended meaning of the Qur'anic revelation by identifying key Qur'anic themes, relating them to the contemporary experience, and piecing them together so as to construct the overall message of the Qur'an.

ETERNAL MESSAGE AND VARYING INTERPRETATIONS

The Qur'an has a definitive message that transcends the historical time and geographical space in which it was revealed. The historical specificity of the community in which it was revealed led to a protracted controversy over the question of the "creation" of the Qur'an. The question of whether the Qur'an was "created" was indeed a question as to whether the Qur'anic message was bound to the historical community that first received it or whether it was transcendental and, hence, relevant to the life of subsequent communities. In the third century of Islam, scholars were divided over the question of the "creation" of the Qur'an; there were those who asserted the historicity of the Qur'an and insisted that it was created—the Mutazilites—and there were those who rejected that assertion, later becoming known as the people of the Sunnah and Community (*ahl al-sunnah wa al-jama'ah*). The conflict between the two groups was theological in nature, involving the relationship between the Book, which was revealed in a particular historical epoch, and its Author, who is eternal and transcends all history.

The theological aspect of the historicity of the Qur'an is no more an issue today, but the exegetical and sociological aspects of the controversy persist. The debate today is over reconciling the claim of the eternity of the Qur'anic message with the fact that the Qur'an was revealed over 1400 years ago to guide a historically situated community. Resolving the issue lies in differentiating between the universal values and transcendental principles which were intended by the Divine to guide the life of a historical community, on the one hand, and the cultural practices and particular social, economic, and political conditions that distinguished the community that received the revealed message, on the other. One has to abstract from the concrete experience of the early Muslim community and use the abstracted knowledge and understanding to guide the experience of modern Muslim society.

The failure to distinguish the intended meaning of the revealed message from the circumstances that prevailed in early Muslim society has led to the rise of literalist interpretations of the Qur'an. The literalist understanding of the Qur'an often confuses the Qur'anic pronouncements against specific actions of the followers of a particular faith community, for instance, with the Qur'an's principled position regarding religious diversity. The Qur'an condemned the unscrupulous behavior of several Jewish tribes toward the Prophet and the then-newly founded Muslim community, in violation of their own religious teachings, while urging Muslims to respect the religious freedom of the Jews and the religious traditions of Judaism.

Contextualizing the Qur'anic verses is, therefore, a must to avoid literalist interpretations. Early Muslim exegesists developed an analytical technique known as *asbab al-nuzul* (reasons of revelation) to understand the meaning of the revealed text in relation to social circumstances. This and other tools of textual analysis have helped avoid literalist interpretations of the text that often distort its intended meaning.

SYSTEMATIC VERSUS SELECTIVE READING

Literalist interpretation is not the only way the intended meaning of the Qur'anic text is distorted. Distortion very often occurs through selective reading of the Qur'an. However, while the selective reading of any text distorts its meaning, the distortion is more possible with regard to the Qur'an, due to the unique Qur'anic presentation. The unique Qur'anic style can be revealed by comparing its account of the creation of man with that of the Bible. Unlike the biblical account, the Qur'an does not present the story of creation through a thematic approach. The story of creation in the Bible can be found in its entirety in the book of Genesis, but it would have to be pursued in different chapters of the Qur'an. The story of creation is narrated in Chapters 2, 3, 7, 15, 17, 18, 19, 26, and 38. The same is true with regard to the missions of the various prophets, the history of the children of Israel, fasting, prayer, and peace and war. This means that a complete and authentic understanding of the Qur'anic text requires a systematic and comprehensive reading of the original text, whereby the interpreter traces the different verses that address the issue at hand. Indeed, the Qur'an itself requires a systematic reading of its message, and it considers any attempt to focus on some verses and ignore others, when dealing with a particular issue, as perversion and distortion (Baqarah 2:85)

Selective reading of the revealed text is wrong because it is an act of deception. Rather than receiving enlightenment and guidance, the selective reader subordinates the divine text to individual inclinations and personal desires. The divine text does not anymore serve as the source of values, beliefs, and guidance but rather is used as a tool for advancing self-interest. Selective reading of the Qur'an reverses the moral order, because it gives priority to the self-interest of the selective reader over universal principles. A person who wants to distort the Qur'anic message to promote a narrow agenda selects the verses that support his position, ignoring other verses that would limit the meaning or application of the selected verses. Thus one finds Muslim extremists marching to the Qur'anic verses that condemn the excesses committed by members of the religious communities that preceded the Islamic revelation, while they overlook the verses that praise the actions of other members of the same communities. By so doing, they advance a position that justifies their open hostility toward Christians and Jews.

Islam's critics in the West unwittingly emulate Muslim extremists when cherry-picking verses from the Qur'an that deal with the theme of struggle and fighting. For example, Robert Spencer, a prolific critic of Islam, has persistently argued that the violence and terrorism employed by Muslim extremists is rooted in the Qur'an and its message. Spencer contends that Muslim extremists who use violence against non-Muslims are not "misrepresenting, twisting, or hijacking what the Qur'an says." "There are over a hundred verses in the Qur'an," he insists, "that exhort believers to wage jihad against unbelievers. 'O Prophet! Strive hard against the unbelievers and the hypocrites, and be firm against them. Their abode is Hell, an evil refuge indeed' (Tawbah 9:73). 'Strive hard' in Arabic is jahidi, a verbal form of the noun jihad. This striving was to be on the battlefield: 'When you meet the unbelievers in the battlefield, strike off their heads and, when you have laid them low, bind your captives firmly' (Muhammad 47:4). This is emphasized repeatedly: 'O you who believe! Fight the unbelievers who gird you about, and let them find firmness in you: and know that God is with those who fear Him' (Tawbah 9:123)."[1]

Spencer picks a few out of numerous verses that deal with issues of peace and war, and he misrepresents Islam by arguing that the Qur'an directs Muslims to fight non-Muslims on the account of having a different faith. He does that by obscuring both the textual and historical contexts of the verses he cites. The Qur'an is unequivocal that fighting is a last resort and is permitted to repulse aggression and stop oppression and abuse: "A declaration of disavowal from God and his messenger to those of the polytheists (Arab pagans) with whom you contracted a mutual alliance" (Tawbah 9:1). The reason for this war against the pagans was their continuous fight and conspiracy against the Muslims, to turn them out of Medina as they had been turned out of Makkah, and their infidelity to and disregard for the covenant they had made with the Muslims: "Why do you not fight people who violated their oaths, plotted to expel the messenger, and attacked you first" (Tawbah 9:13). Out of the hundreds of Qur'anic verses left out of Spencer's discussion are those that direct Muslims to initiate fighting only to repel aggression, while urging them to

[1]Robert Spencer, "Jihadism and the Qur'an," *Front Page Magazine,* December 8, 2005.

seek peace when the other party seeks peace: "Fight in the way of God those who fight you, but do not commit aggression, for God loves not aggressors. And fight them wherever you meet them, and turn them out from where they have turned you out; for persecution is worse than slaughter. But if they cease, God is oft-forgiving, most merciful. And fight them on until there is no oppression and the religion is only for God, but if they cease, let there be no hostility except to those who practice oppression" (Baqarah 2:190–193).

THE MESSAGE OF THE QUR'AN

Does the Qur'an have a clear and consistent message for its readers? And if the answer is in the affirmative, what is this message?

The debate over whether the Qur'an has a clear and consistent message has raged for over a millennium, even among Muslim scholars. Many renowned Muslim jurists argued that the Qur'an is open to many interpretations (*hamal awjuh*). This widely held opinion about the Qur'an emboldened the *hadith* jurists (*muhadithun*), who have persistently relied on *hadith* books to develop Islamic theology, ethics, and eschatology.

In modern times, the Qur'an has been frequently referenced by Muslim intellectuals and scholars to advance ideas and interpretations of varying emphases. The Qur'an is presented by contemporary authors as providing a spiritual, scientific, political, and even revolutionary message. The fact that the Qur'an has been presented in competing lights reaffirms the old argument that it is open to different interpretations. Openness to interpretation is a quality that is characteristic of all revealed books, indeed of all books dealing with matters of considerable depth. Yet, asserting that the Qur'an can mean different things to different people does not mean that one must concede that the Qur'an does not carry a clear and definitive message to its readers.

The Qur'an has indeed a clear and definitive message, and this message, as I attempt to illustrate throughout this book, is one of peace, harmony, and hope. The Qur'an urges its readers to seek a life of peace—peace with oneself, peace with God, peace with other human beings with whom one is constantly interacting, and peace with the larger social and natural environment. This book is, therefore, divided into 27 chapters addressing the major themes of the Qur'an. The various Qur'anic themes are subsumed under six grand themes: Spirit, Faith, Inner Peace, Community Peace, Universal Peace, and Eternal Peace.

Peace, as presented in the Qur'an, is not the premise upon which human life is constructed but the general goal and the final end to which life should evolve. The road to peace is, though, a tedious and challenging journey that starts with discovering the spiritual essence of life. Listening to the spiritual voice and choosing God and his guidance over the immediate demands of the world lead the individual to a life of faith, the cornerstone of peace. Through faith the human spirit finds its way to inner peace, as the first step in the journey to eternal peace. In the movement from inner to eternal peace lies the purpose of life and the mission of humanity. Man was created, the Qur'an teaches, to fulfill a divine purpose by bringing the latent human qualities of intelligence and passion to bear on the social and natural environments in which the human being finds himself or herself. In the struggle to fulfill the divine intent of creation, the human spirit has to struggle to find its eternal peace by seeking communal and universal peace. Struggle is then the way to attain peace. The struggle is multidimensional and is never perfect or complete, but rather it always evolves around key concepts and values. The key to moral perfection, the Qur'an stresses, is moral discipline and a strong commitment to justice and to a life of equity and balance. Death ultimately concludes the human endeavor to find peace and harmony in the world and brings the human being face to face with eternity and the prospect of eternal peace.

I attempt in this book to spell out the overall message of the Qur'an by exploring key Qur'anic themes. While I tried carefully to choose the themes and put them together to develop an overall message, I am quite aware of my individual and historical limitations. I do fully realize that what comes out of this exercise is not the definitive Qur'anic message but an approximation of it that must be continuously revised, developed, and completed by the contribution of other scholars and readers of the Qur'an.

PART I

SPIRIT

Spirit is the most intricate element of being, for it is both the source and culmination of existence. Through the spirit the world receives its meaning and purpose, and through it enlightenment, wisdom, growth, beauty, glory, and elegance can be experienced.

Yet the spirit remains the most mysterious element of existence and continues to defy all efforts to decipher its truth. This is what the Qur'an has to say about the spirit:

> They ask you concerning the spirit. Say: The spirit is of the order of my Lord: of knowledge it is only a little that is communicated to you.
>
> (Isra' 17:85)

Despite all the advances humanity has achieved in understanding matter, little progress has been made in understanding the spirit. The quality that makes us the intelligent and passionate beings that we are, which we call "spirit," is the least apprehended concept of the human understanding. The above verse remains true in spite of all the scientific developments humanity has experienced since its revelation.

The Qur'an does not, though, leave us clueless in our endeavors to understand the spirit and spirituality. It first tells us that the human spirit emanates directly from the divine spirit. The affinity of the human to the Divine is spiritual, and hence the human spirit is the enduring link that brings the human being close to his or her divine origin.

Part I focuses on capturing glimpses of both the human spirit and that of the Divine, and it explores the spiritual connection between the two.

CHAPTER 1

Origin and Purpose

The purpose of human creation is the most important question that continuously confronts every living soul, and the question is directly linked to that of the origin of life. The two questions are among the most contentious issues we confront, and they are the most difficult to clarify.

What is the source of human life, and what is its final end? Does life have a purpose, and if it does, how is this purpose relevant to the overall existence? What is the relationship between the human body and soul, and are they separable? These are some of the questions we will explore in this chapter by focusing on the Qur'anic narrative of the origin and purpose of life.

HUMAN BODY

All of us come to consciousness in complex natural and social orders. We are part of a boundless natural order. The universe appears from the human vantage point as limitless space, both at the macro and micro levels. Our current knowledge of our cosmic surroundings points to an ordered universe. The cosmos is made of countless celestial objects orbiting around countless stars, ordered into countless galaxies, and vanishing into countless black holes. The cosmos with its staggering size and endless varieties is equally limitless at the microcosm. Humans have been able to refine their observation tools, and we have found that the matter that fills the universe is so diverse and so minute in its structure that its building blocks cannot be directly observed by our most powerful microscopes.

Our social surrounding is equally diverse and complex. No human has ever had the opportunity to witness the beginning of human life. We are members of a species whose origin is counted by tens—if not hundreds—of thousands of years. There are many narratives as to how human life came to being that can be ultimately subsumed under two grand narratives: creation and evolution. Evolution is widely embraced by natural scientists who attempt to reconstruct the beginning of human life by tracing prehistoric animal life, finding in the shared biological traits of all living creatures evidence of common ancestry and common evolution. For them, human life evolved from the general animal life through a process of natural selection.

Followers of monotheistic religions share a grand narrative that places the beginning of human life with the creation of the first masculine human being, Adam, along with his feminine spouse. The Qur'an describes human creation by narrating an exchange between God and the angels:

> Behold, your Lord said to the angels: I am about to create man from clay: when I have fashioned him (in due proportion) and breathed into him of my Spirit, fall down unto him.
>
> (Sad 38:71–72)

A similar narration is provided in another Qur'anic verse with a slightly modified description. In this more elaborate account, the clay from which the human body is shaped goes through some organic transformation, as it turns into smelly and darkened clay:

> Behold! Your Lord said to the angels: I am about to create man, from dark malodorous clay, from mud molded into shape; when I have fashioned him (in due proportion) and breathed into him of my Spirit, fall you down unto him.
>
> (Hijr 15:28–29)

The human being, according to the Qur'an, is made of earthly matter, mixed with water and left for a while until it has gone through a process of transformation. The clay from which man was created had already gone through a transformation of sorts, to become malodorous clay having a dark color, thereby suggesting an organic process. The clay was then molded into the human shape, into which the Divine breathed, imbuing it with a spirit derived from his own.

The Qur'an is silent as to the nature of the process through which the human body took its final shape. Was the human body created instantaneously, or did it go through an evolutionary process? What is clear, though, is that the Qur'an places the question of the origin of life within the realm of natural observation rather than theoretical reflection. That is, investigating human creation belongs to scientific observation and not to theology.

> Say: Travel through the earth and see how God did originate creation; so will God produce a later creation: for God has power over all things.
>
> ('Ankabut 29:20)

Yet the Qur'an describes in so many different ways human creation as an elaborate and phased process, whereby the human being goes through various phases before it evolves into the human shape. The above verses of Chapter 15 refer to a process of "molding into shape" or *taswiyah* that culminates in the human creation. In Chapter 7, the Qur'an refers to the two phases of human creation—the act of creation and the process of shaping:

> It is we who created you then gave you shape; then we bade the angels bow down to Adam, and they bowed down; not so Iblis (Lucifer); he refused to be of those who bow down.
>
> (A'raf 7:11)

Indeed, the Qur'anic description of human creation suggests an evolutionary process, whereby human life evolves through distinct stages and takes different forms. It begins with the most primordial stages of organic transformation of soil and continues through various stages in the mother's womb, followed by several phases of development, from infancy to full adulthood, to senility for those who reach very advanced age; and finally it ends with death.

> O mankind! If you have a doubt about the resurrection, (consider) that we created you out of dust, then out of sperm, then out of a leech-like clot, then out of a morsel of flesh, partly formed and partly unformed, in order that we may manifest (our power) to you; and we cause whom we will to rest in the wombs for an appointed term, then do we bring you out as babies, then (foster you) that you may reach your age of full strength; and some of you are called to die, and some are sent back to the feeblest old age, so that they know nothing after having known (much). And (further), you see the earth barren and lifeless, but when we pour down rain on it, it is stirred (to life), it swells, and it puts forth every kind of beautiful growth in pairs.
>
> (Hajj 22:5)

In this account, one sees clearly an evolutionary process of creation, in which life starts with dust, and then evolves into a single cell (sperm) that multiplies to form a clot (*'alaqah*), which grows into bone and finally to flesh. It is interesting that while the process referred to here mainly describes the growth of the fetus in the mother's womb, the Qur'an starts its description of the fetus's growth by referring to the earthly dust, thereby suggesting a comparable evolutionary process that was part of the act of creation of the first human being. This suggestion is further enforced by the conclusion of the verse, where the Qur'an invokes the ever-observable process of rejuvenation of vegetation in the desert during the annual rain season. The return of life to an apparently lifeless desert after receiving heavy rain is a gradual and relatively slow process associated with the growth of vegetation.

And while the Qur'an describes a purposive act of creation of human beings, the account it gives does not exclude an evolutionary biological process leading to the completion and physical maturation of the human being. What sets human and animal lives apart, according to the Qur'an, is not primarily the biological development of the human body, but the moral, intellectual, and spiritual capacity of the human spirit. Human life enjoys dignity that is unique to the human being, dignity that is rooted in human spirituality, not biology.

HUMAN SPIRIT

Human life stands out from other forms of life by qualities that emanate directly from the divine spirit. Emulating the divine spirit, human spirit is endowed with the qualities of knowledge, justice, compassion, wisdom, peace, love, creativity, patience, gratefulness, and the like. These qualities empower the human being to assume the most honored mission in the entire creation, of being the divine vicegerent (*khalifah*) on earth. Humanity has been given mastery over the earthly domain and is entrusted with developing this domain by developing its collective presence.

> Behold, your Lord said to the angels: I will create a vicegerent on earth. They said: Will you place therein one who will make mischief and shed blood, while we do celebrate your praises and glorify your holy name? He said: I know what you know not.
>
> (Baqarah 2:30)

This exchange that took place right before the creation of Adam reveals both the purpose of human life and the apprehension the angels had about the creation of human beings that were destined to shed blood and make mischief on earth. The above verse affirms in one breath that the human being, whose qualities derive directly from those of the Divine, is commissioned to give care to the earthly domain, and, at the same time, is susceptible to committing excesses by making mischief and shedding blood. This fact was a source of a great concern to the angels, whose outstanding quality was a deep sense of obedience and loyalty to the Divine.

The divine response was not to refute the angels' misgivings about human excesses, but to reveal the special quality of the last intelligent creature to come to life in the universe: conceptual learning and knowledge. Humans, the Qur'an tells us, have the capacity to recognize objects and the ability to assign to them appropriate labels or names.

> And he [God] taught Adam the names of all things; then he placed them before the angels, and said: Tell me the names of these if you are right. They said: Glory to you: of knowledge we have none, save what you have taught us: in truth it is you who are perfect in knowledge and wisdom. He said: O Adam! Tell them their names. When he had told them, God said: Did I not

tell you that I know the secrets of heavens and earth, and I know what you reveal and what you conceal?

(Baqarah 2:31–33)

In responding to the divine commandment to bow down to Adam, the angels obliged willingly, but not so did the avowed enemy of man—Satan.

And behold, we said to the angels: Bow down to Adam. And they bowed down. Not so Iblis, he refused and was arrogant: he was of those who reject faith.

(Baqarah 2:24)

In justifying his refusal to bow down to Adam and comply with the divine command, Iblis, the devil, presented the first racist argument: "I am better than he," he asserted:

(God) said: What prevented you from bowing down when I commanded you? He said: I am better than he; you created me from fire and created him from clay.

(A'raf 7:12)

Both the angels and Iblis objected to the creation of the first human being. However, while the angels focused on the negative aspects of human experience as the basis for their objection, and quickly reconciled themselves with the elevated mission of humans, Iblis was exceedingly self-centered. His objection was based on a comparison that focused exclusively on physical qualities. Henceforth, Satan declared himself an eternal enemy to humanity and vowed to prove that human beings are not worthy of the divine trust.

(God) said: Then get you out from here: for you are rejected, accursed. And my curse shall be on you till the day of judgment. (Iblis) said: O my Lord! Give me then respite till the day the (dead) are raised. (God) said: Respite then is granted to you till the day of the time appointed. (Iblis) said: Then, by your power, I will put them all in the wrong—except your servants amongst them, sincere and purified (by your grace). (God) said: Then it is just and fitting—and I say what is just and fitting that I will certainly fill hell with you and those that follow you—every one.

(Sad 38:78–85)

With the open enmity expressed by Iblis toward humanity, the human mission to serve the Divine became clearer. Man has to apply his innate qualities to his earthly environment and use his acquired power in ways that improve the overall human condition and uplift the human spirit. This will have to begin with maintaining self-discipline and self-control and overcoming the temptations and the lure of Iblis. The first human beings had to learn this important fact the hard way. The setting for the first lesson is the Garden, where Adam and Eve had a firsthand experience with temptation and Satanic lure.

We said: O Adam! Dwell and your wife in the garden; and eat of the bounti-
ful things therein as (where and when) you will; but approach not this tree,
or you run into harm and transgression. Then did Satan make them slip from
the (garden), and get them out of the state (of felicity) in which they had
been. We said: Get down all with enmity between yourselves. On earth will
be your dwelling-place and your means of livelihood—for a time.

(Baqarah 2:35–36)

THE MISSION

The human being is commissioned to be the trustee of the earthly
domain—the moral agent who applies innate human qualities to make
the world a better place and to use the tremendous resources that were
placed in the human trust. Human resources, the Qur'an tells us, are as
limitless as the universe that nurtures and surrounds human life.

Do you not see that God has subjected to your (use) all things in the heavens
and on earth, and has made his bounties flow to you in exceeding measure,
(both) seen and unseen? Yet there are among humans those who dispute
about God, without knowledge and without guidance, and without a book
to enlighten them!

(Luqman 31:20)

This observation by Luqman the wise, often repeated in the Qur'an,
points to the great potential of humanity to harness the power of the universe and use it for accomplishing humanity's mission. Through the
power of knowledge, human beings received the most important mission
in the entire creation—to be the trustees of the most colorful and deco-
rated planet. To carry on the mission effectively, humanity must keep in
touch with its source and must commit itself to the universal principles
of right, justice, and compassion, in order to bring discipline and direction
to human endeavors. This constant engagement with the source of life
and the subordination of individual follies to universal truth is the true
essence of service and worship required of all creatures, particularly
those who have the ability to go astray.

I have only created *jinns* and humans that they may serve me.

(Dhariyat 51:56)

Each of the three intelligent species that exist in the universe must
serve and worship God in a manner consistent with its own mission.
The angels, made of light and having the capacity to move swiftly
between heaven and earth, are given the mission of taking care of, and
maintaining, the universal order. They respond willingly to every divine
directive. They never desire anything contrary to the divine command.

O you who believe! Save yourselves and your families from a fire whose fuel
is men and stones, over which are (appointed) angels stern (and) severe, who

flinch not (from executing) the commands they receive from God, but do (precisely) what they are commanded.

(Tahrim 66:6)

Jinns (devils), made of fire, are capable of influencing humans by whispering their ideas and thoughts; they are apparently deprived of any power to translate their wishes and hopes into reality on their own—they can do that, however, through human agency. It is this capability that led Iblis to pledge to lure people into wrongdoing, except those who are given to remembrance and obedience of God. Some of the *jinns,* the Qur'an asserts, obey God, while others rebel against the divine command, in the manner of Satan.

The rebellious *jinns* have vowed to drive humanity into rebellion, hence the divine command to humans to take the party of Iblis as enemies:

Behold! We said to the angels: Bow down to Adam. They bowed down except Iblis. He was one of the *jinns,* and he broke the command of his Lord. Will you then take him and his progeny as friends and protectors rather than me? And they are enemies to you! Evil would be the exchange for the wrongdoers!

(Kahf 18:50)

The human being consists of a unique combination of the solid matter of the universe along with the divine spirit that stems directly from God. Humans have many of the attributes of the Divine, albeit in a finite form. They have been given intelligence, the power of choice, and the ability to translate their choices into reality within the earthly domain.

To be truthful to their purpose and mission, humans must serve God and embrace his will. They must pursue truth, right, and justice, and they must develop moral discipline and self-control so they do not commit excesses and succumb to temptation. And herein lies the challenge facing humanity, and the constant need to maintain connections with their divine source.

CHAPTER 2

Divine Presence

Understanding the mystery of human life takes us on a journey to explore the source of life—the Divine. Yet understanding divinity is more challenging for human reason than comprehending human life. For the Divine, as the Qur'an describes him, is both the beginning and end, the inner and the outer, and the imminent and transcendent.

MOST BEAUTIFUL NAMES

The Qur'an refers to God using the masculine pronoun "him." This reference does not, however, indicate gender, for the category of gender is contrary to the Qur'anic conception of the Divine. For God, the Qur'an stresses, is the one being who has nothing comparable to him:

> Say: He is God, the One; God, the Self-sustaining; he begets not, nor is he begotten; and there is none like unto him.
>
> (Ikhlas 112:1–4)

Having no equivalence, no one who is like him, does not mean the Divine is unknowable. God reveals himself in the Qur'an in ways that make him quite comprehensible to humans, for his attributes resonate with the human spirit:

> God is he, beside whom there is no other god; he knows (all things) both secret and open; he, Most Gracious, Most Merciful. God is he, beside whom there is no other god; the Sovereign, the Holy, the Peace, the Guardian of Faith, the Preserver of Safety, the Exalted in Might, the Irresistible, the Supreme: glory to God! (High is he) above the partners they attribute to him. He is God, the Creator, the Evolver, the Bestower of Forms. To him belong the most beautiful names: whatever is in the heavens and on earth, does celebrate his praises and glory: and he is the Exalted in Might, the Wise.
>
> (Hashr 59:22–24)

God is known to Muslims through his "beautiful names" (*al-asma' al-husna*), his personal attributes that at the same time are familiar to humans because human beings share similar qualities, albeit in finite forms. Muslim scholars have identified 99 divine attributes by examining how God describes himself in the Qur'an. Here is a selected list of the names of God showing his divine attributes:

The One, the Holy, the Merciful, the Compassionate, the Forgiving, the Peace, the Just, the Living, the Loving, the Light, the Guide, the Gentle, the Faithful, the Grateful, the Imminent, the Manifest, the First, the Last, the Knowing, the Wise, the Prudent, the Patient, the Enduring, the Forbearing, the Listener, the Observer, the Watchful, the Witness, the Creator, the Innovator, the Giver, the Caretaker, the Provider, the Protector, the Sustainer, the Powerful, the Overpowering, the Invincible, the Mighty, the Sublime, the Generous, the Glorious, the Inventor, the Sustainer, the Self-Expanding, the Fashioner, the Conqueror, the Omniscient, the Judge, the Equitable, the Gracious, the Clement, the Exalted, the Great, the Responder, the Truth, the Trustee, the Almighty, the Praiseworthy, the Originator, the Life-Giver, the Effector of Death, the Restorer, the Self-Subsisting, the Self-Righteous, the Avenger, the Pardoner, the Kind, the Patron, the Rich, the Enricher, the Benefactor, the Incomparable, the Inheritor.

THE ORDER OF INFINITY AND FINITUDE

The fact that divine attributes are also human qualities does not mean that humans can fully appreciate the transformation these attribute undergo when they move from the infinite to the finite. This meaning has been clearly expressed in various Qur'anic verses:

> No just estimate have they made of God, such as is due to him: on the day of judgment the whole of the earth will be but his handful, and the heavens will be rolled up in his right hand: glory to him! High is he above the partners they attribute to him!
>
> (Zumar 39:67)

Not only the magnitude of power is different, but the way divine power manifests itself in relation to other divine attributes puts divine acts on a completely different order. Human limitation makes it necessary for actors to gather information, examine the availability of resources, and develop the necessary tools for performing the act. Any gap between the human will and the necessary requirements for the realization of the act affects negatively the ability of human beings to making their will a reality. The distance between intentions and actions immediately disappears in the divine order. For at this level all it takes for something to happen is for it to be willed:

Verily, when he intends a thing, his command is be, and it is!

(Yasin 36:82)

The complete accord between divine intention and action does not, however, negate temporal and spatial dimensions of existence. Divine actions take place through time and space. The creation of the heavens and the earth transpired over time, as the Qur'an tells us that it took six days to complete. The days are naturally of a divine order, and are markedly different from earthly days. The Qur'an provides an example of the enormous difference between the earthly and heavenly days, in reference to the time it takes for divine decree to manifest on earth:

He rules (all) affairs from the heavens to the earth: in the end will (all affairs) go up to him, on a day, the space whereof is (as) a thousand years of your reckoning.

(Sajdah 32:5)

Time and space also affect the rhythm of the movement of angels who are entrusted with maintaining various aspects of the universal order, thereby reaffirming the affinity of time-space to the divine order.

The angels and the Spirit ascend unto him in a day the measure whereof is (as) fifty thousand years.

(Ma'arij 70:4)

Again, although all it takes for something to take place is to be willed by the Divine, this does not mean that the divine will is arbitrary or lacks structure. The divine will is structured and ordered, and for that reason the universe is an orderly place. The Qur'an repeatedly points to the precision in the movement of the sun and the moon, and it stresses that every thing in the universe exists in accordance with precise measures.

The universal order, the Qur'an tells us, is patterned in accordance to an internal necessity, so that, for example, the sun's orbit must not deviate in any way that would interfere with the moon's orbit. But the necessity of the universal order is only internal; that is, it is intended to ensure certain universal conditions that are necessary for earthly life. There is nothing that can prevent the current order from being changed and replaced with a completely different order, as will be, the Qur'an asserts, the case in the life to come. The Qur'an stresses that on the day of resurrection, the current universal order will disappear to give way to one that is suitable to the eternal life:

The day that we roll up the heavens like a scroll rolled up for books (completed), as we started the first creation, so shall we bring it back anew: a promise we have undertaken: truly shall we fulfill it.

(Anbiya' 21:104)

The Qur'an states clearly that the act of destroying the current order and bringing back to life every human being who has ever lived on earth is a necessary act, born out of self-imposed commitment on the part of the creator. The divine will and the divine order combine in an extraordinary way the principles of freedom and necessity. The divine will is free, but divine freedom embraces necessity, either in the form of orderly, structured divine acts, or in self-imposed commitments. The latter can be seen in God's commitment to act in accordance to the principle of mercy:

> Say: To whom belongs all that is in the heavens and on earth? Say: To God. He has prescribed for himself (the rule of) mercy. That he will gather you together for the day of judgment, there is no doubt whatever. It is they who have lost their own souls that will not believe.
>
> (An'am 6:12)

SPIRITUALLY CONNECTED AND ENGAGING DIVINE

Perhaps with the exception of "self-sustaining" and "life-giver," all other divine attributes can be observed in human forms. The difference of course is humongous. It is the difference of having any of the above qualities in a finite and the Infinite. Of course, the shared qualities result from the very divine breath into the human body that brought humanity to life.

Using a metaphoric language to help people grasp the enormous difference, the Prophet provided a parable for the divine quality of compassion:

> On the authority of Abu Hurayra that the Prophet, peace and mercy on him, said: God has divided his compassion to a hundred portions, he kept 99 portions with him and sent down one to the earth; from that part all creatures display mercy, so that the horse exerts utmost care to avoid running her offspring down.
>
> (Reported by Tirmidhi)

The distance between the human and the Divine in power and capacity has created a conceptual distance between man and God, and has led a great many people to stay aloof from their source. It takes only a quick glance through the heavenly distances to bring the human being to see his humble capacity and reach in relation with the creator and sustainer of the universe.

The Greeks' mechanical understanding of the universe led them to perceive God as the first cause, a distant being who set the universe in motion at a distant past and then left it alone to its own means.

Early theological writings that were influenced by the Greek conception of the Divine presented God in a similar light. Understanding the relationship of God to his creation through the work of many theologians would lead one to believe that God's involvement with his creation ended with the completion of creation of the universe and life therein, signified by God's ascending to the throne on the seventh day of creation.

The Qur'an describes the relationship of God to the universe in general, and human life in particular, in more intimate and engaging ways. The Qur'an reminds us of a very basic fact that tends to be lost when God is perceived from a purely human vantage point.

Humans, by virtue of having spirits that emanate from the Divine, engage in acts of creation by molding various objects of the earth into shapes in line with particular concepts and functions. Humans are not linked in any organic or spiritual way with the objects they create or produce. Upon completing their creative work, they can leave the object and move on, but still the objects they create persist and function in their absence.

This is not, however, the relationship of the Divine to his creation. It is quite startling to human understanding to realize, as the Qur'an reminds us, that God's creation cannot persist, not even for a moment, without being continuously willed and cared for by the Divine. God, the Qur'an stresses, is not merely the first cause, but a caring, engaging creator:

> Or, who listens to the (soul) distressed when it calls on him, and who relieves its suffering, and makes you (humans) inheritors of the earth? (Can there be another) god besides God? Little it is that you heed! Or, who guides you through the depths of darkness on land and sea, and who sends the winds as heralds of glad tidings, going before his mercy? (Can there be another) god besides God? High is God above what they associate with him! Or, who originates creation, then repeats it, and who gives you sustenance from heaven and earth? (Can there be another) god besides God? Say: Bring forth your argument, if you are telling the truth!
>
> (Naml 27:62–64)

In a most fundamental way, the continuation of life and existence itself is only possible because the divine attributes are continuously brought to bear on the universe. The universe is completely dependant on the continuous caring of God:

> It is God who holds the heavens and the earth, lest they perish; and they would surely perish, if anyone other than him held them thereafter: verily he is most forbearing, oft-forgiving.
>
> (Fatir 35:41)

So the universe, and every life therein, will cease, should the Divine withhold its care and support from it. The universe literally emanates from the divine will and qualities. It is in constant needs for the care, sustenance, and providence of the Divine. It is, therefore, the manifestation of divine attributes and qualities. Knowing the creation should lead to knowing the creator. The universe and human life are rich with the signs (*ayahs*) that lead to the Divine:

Soon will we show them our signs in the (farthest) regions (of the earth), and
in their own souls, until it becomes manifest to them that this is the truth. Is it
not enough that your Lord does witness all things?

(Fussilat 41:53)

One can also be guided to the creator by observing human life, both on
the individual and collective levels. On the individual level, the Divine
can be appreciated by observing the knowledge, wisdom, justice, and
compassion displayed by human beings. For, like the case of compassion
referred to above, human knowledge, wisdom, and justice reveal bits and
pieces of divine knowledge, wisdom, and justice, and they provide clues
of the greatness of God as they point consciousness toward its majestic
source.

One can also turn inside and look into his own life situation and his
own soul. The hands of God that guide and protect are made apparent at
every juncture of individual life, particularly for those who often remember God, seek his pleasure and support, and struggle to follow his wisdom
and guidance. The voice that brings the human being to open up and reach
out to the Divine is deep in the human spirit. After all, it is only by reconnecting to its source that the finite spirit of man can find its fulfillment. For
as long as the human spirit has not been completely cut from its source
through multiple layers of mischief, arrogance, selfishness, and injustice,
the human spirit can discern the presence of the Divine, for he is closer
to any human being than his or her own jugular vein:

It was we who created man, and we know what dark suggestions his soul
makes to him: for we are nearer to him than (his) jugular vein.

(Qaf 50:16)

Then why do you not (intervene) when (the soul of the dying man) reaches
the throat, and you the while (sit) looking on, but we are nearer to him than
you, and yet you realize not.

(Waqi'ah 56:83–85)

DIVINE PRESENCE IN HISTORY

God did not create humanity and then abandon it to its own means.
The Qur'an tells us that God cares about human life and human history,
and is actively engaged to ensure that truth prevails over falsehood and
that justice has the upper hand over corruption and oppression. Given
the complete free will granted to human beings, God ensures that falsehood and corruption are repeatedly defeated by truth and justice.

God stands behind those who are committed to goodness, right, and
justice. This does not, however, mean that his support is exclusive to particular religious or ethnic groups, but it is rather based on intentions and
actions, as well as on the balance of goodness and power.

What! When a single disaster smites you, although you smote (your enemies) with one twice as great, do you say? Whence is this? Say (to them): It is from yourselves: for God has power over all things.

(Al 'Imran 3:156)

Of the bounties of your Lord we bestow freely on all these as well as those: the bounties of your Lord are not closed (to anyone).

(Isra' 17:20)

Although people enjoy complete freedom to choose their course of action, people are not always able to achieve the goals they set out to accomplish. For human history illustrates that only actions that benefit humanity at large leave a lasting impression on subsequent generations, while selfish acts that are of personal benefit are quickly forgotten and leave no positive impact in society.

He sends down water from the skies, and the channels flow, each according to its measure: but the torrent bears away the foam that mounts up to the surface. Even so, from that (ore) which they heat in the fire, to make ornaments or utensils therewith, there is a scum likewise. Thus does God (by parables) show forth truth and vanity. For the scum disappears like froth cast out; while that which is for the good of humanity remains on the earth. Thus does God set forth parables.

(Ra'd 13:17)

Again, God is not a passive observer in the struggle between good and evil, but an active participant who takes the side of goodness and undermines the work of evil, always in ways that turn mean-spirited plots against those who are planning them:

Remember how the unbelievers plotted against you, to keep you in bonds, or slay you, or get you out (of your home). They plot and plan, and God too plans, but the best of planners is God.

(Anfal 8:30)

Those driven by greed and lust for power soon get disappointed. They quickly discover that their plots to advance their own selfish interests at the expense of others are far from watertight, and that the unintended consequences of their actions overwhelm their unscrupulous efforts.

The unbelievers spend their wealth to hinder (men) from the path of God, and so will they continue to spend; but in the end they will have (only) regrets and sighs; at length they will be overcome: and the unbelievers will be gathered together to hell.

(Anfal 8:36)

Might does not make right, for as soon as a generation decides to use the might it acquired from the hard work of many generations preceding it, it unwittingly undermines its power in the course of pursuing unscrupulous ends. In the struggle between social forces, those who intend to promote the greater good are always triumphant, while those who intend to promote the interests of the few at the expense of the greater multitude bring destruction and defeat to their ranks.

While the Qur'an asserts that the struggle between good and evil is the motor that drives human history, it rejects the view that societies and communities are divided neatly around these concepts. Rather, the Qur'an provides a more complex picture in which good and evil often coexist in the same human setting:

> They are the ones who denied revelation and hindered you from the Sacred Mosque and the sacrificial animals, detained from reaching their place of sacrifice. Had there not been believing men and believing women whom you did not know that you were trampling down and on whose account a crime would have accrued to you without (your) knowledge, (God would have allowed you to force your way, but he held back your hands) that he may admit to his mercy whom he will. If they had been apart, we should certainly have punished the unbelievers among them with a grievous punishment.
>
> (Fath 48:25)

> But God was not going to send them a penalty whilst you were amongst them; nor was he going to send it whilst they do ask for pardon.
>
> (Anfal 8:33)

So the Divine in the Qur'an is living, loving, compassionate, and engaging. He cares about human life, and he provides guidance and support to those who seek truth and justice. His qualities are not fragmented as in the case of the human being. For humans, the qualities of compassion, justice, and wisdom are potential qualities that need to be nurtured and nourished though self-discipline and commitment. They often require a system of checks and balances so that individual excesses are checked by other individuals and by institutions. But those diverse qualities coexist in the Divine in a perfect balance. For unlike humans, God has those qualities in equal abundance of infinity.

CHAPTER 3

Prophets of Transcendence

Prophets have historically been essential for realigning the human spirit with its divine origin every time humans strayed away from their moral source and indulged themselves in social excesses. When God brought the first two human beings, Adam and Eve, along with the first *jinn*, Iblis (Lucifer), down to dwell on earth, he promised them guidance. The guidance came down every time people distorted the divine message and deformed their social conditions, giving rise to corruption and injustice. The message came through human messengers who reintroduced truth to the people and led them on a reform mission.

All the prophets who received divine inspiration and revelation were selected to perform the difficult but important mission of delivering humanity back to a life of truth, and of helping people transcend their individual and egotistic limitations. The reason for selecting a particular person to be commissioned as a prophet is not fully explained in the Qur'an. One common denominator, though, is that prophets were always distinguished by an outstanding character and deep devotion to God. They were all distinguished by a strong yearning for the Divine. They were authentic human beings vividly aware that they grew in communities that had gone astray, and they were on a pathfinding mission to reconnect with their spiritual origin, to reconnect with the transcendental God. They all displayed deep compassion for fellow humans, particularly the less fortunate. The truth they brought always called for the leveling of the playfield by ensuring fairness and equity, and by advancing social justice.

THE PRINCIPLE OF *TAWHID*

Nowhere is devotion to God and the values and principles associated with him clearer than in the life of Ibrahim (Abraham), the one who is accredited by the Qur'an for planting the principle of *tawhid* (the unity of the transcendental God) in an actual human community.

Like Prophet Muhammad, Ibrahim grew up in a community that practiced idolatry. He came to faith after a long and difficult journey, which started in a genuine search for the source of life and truth. Ibrahim started his journey to faith by looking up to heaven and searching for the true God:

> Lo! Ibrahim said to his father Azar: Do you take idols for gods? For I do indeed see that you and your people are in manifest error. So also did we show Ibrahim the power and the laws of the heavens and the earth, that he might (with understanding) have certitude. When the night covered him over, he saw a star and said: This is my lord. But when it set, he said: I love not those that set. When he saw the moon rising in splendor, he said: This is my lord. But when the moon set, he said: Unless my lord guides me, I shall surely be among those who go astray.
>
> (An'am 6:74–77)

Ultimately, he came to realize through his search for the Divine that the latter cannot dwell in any part of his creation, and must transcend all, for he is the source, the creator.

> When he saw the sun rising in splendor, he said: This is my lord; this is the greatest (of all). But when the sun set, he said: O my people! I am indeed free from your (guilt) of giving partners to God. For me, I have set my face, firmly and truly, towards him who created the heavens and the earth, and never shall I give partners to God.
>
> (An'am 6:78–79)

Ibrahim's embrace of the principle of *tawhid* was not simply an intellectual recognition of the oneness and unity of the Divine, but a complete submission to the divine will, and a full acceptance of his commandments. Ibrahim was willing to obey God and accept his decrees even when this meant that he may have to sacrifice his own flesh and blood, the son he dearly loved.

Ibrahim's commitment to God put him on a journey of great challenges that began with his community's attempt to burn him alive after he challenged their false beliefs. He lived a long life in the Holy Land, in which he sought refuge after escaping an almost certain death. Evidently, Ibrahim's strong faith in the transcendental God did not spread beyond his family, and when he died much of the world around him was not aware of him and his life struggle. Paradoxically, Ibrahim's life was one of the most influential lives in the history of humanity. The two children, Ishmael and Isaac, he left behind, to whom he bequeathed a profound faith in the one God, founded the two communities that would ultimately nurture Judaism, Christianity, and Islam.

Ibrahim is undoubtedly the founder of the monotheistic tradition, the tradition of *tawhid*. To his wisdom, devotion, and courage all the communities of faith are indebted; in his tradition all the prophets were schooled. Despite the long line of prophets who came in between the mission of Prophet Ibrahim and that of Prophet Muhammad, the latter was directed to embrace the faith of the former in clear recognition of the essential role Ibrahim played in founding the true faith.

> And now we have revealed to you our will, saying: Follow the faith of Ibrahim the upright, he joined not gods with God.
>
> (Nahl 16:123)

TRANSCENDENTAL MESSAGES DELIVERED BY HUMAN PROPHETS

The guidance that God promised to send to earth was always delivered through human messengers. The humanness of the prophets was frequently the ground for being initially rejected by their communities, and the social status of the prophets was often questioned. Pharaoh, for instance, rejected the prophetic mission of Musa (Moses), and reminded him of the favors of the house of pharaohs on him. Jesus was, similarly, rejected by the religious establishment of his community. Jesus was never schooled in the rabbinic tradition and was never certified as a rabbi, and hence he was not granted the religious authority to interpret the Torah. Both Moses and Jesus were given the power to perform miracles as a means to certify their divine mission.

The divine message delivered by the prophets, the Qur'an tells us, was often rejected because the messengers were always humans. The humanness of the prophets, the Qur'an asserts, was intended for a very obvious reason: the only way for humans to interact with any messenger sent by the Divine, whether that messenger is truly human or not, is for the messenger to assume a human form.

> What kept men back from belief when guidance came to them, was nothing but this: they said: Has God sent a man (like us) to be (his) messenger? Say: If there were settled, on earth, angels walking about in peace and quiet, we should certainly have sent them down from the heavens an angel for a messenger.
>
> (Isra' 17:94–95)

> They say: Why is not an angel sent down to him? If we did send down an angel, the matter would be settled at once, and no respite would be granted them. If we had made it an angel, we should have sent him as a man, and we should certainly have caused them to wear of the things they themselves wear.
>
> (An'am 6:8–9)

The humanness of the prophets was also intended so that their followers could see them as role models to be emulated. This would not be the case if the messengers had different qualities than the recipients of the message.

And they say: What sort of a messenger is this, who eats foods, and walks through the streets? Why has not an angel been sent down to him to give admonition with him?

(Furqan 25:7)

Like all the prophets who preceded him, Prophet Muhammad came to reassert the essential message of *tawhid*— acknowledging the oneness of God and submitting to the divine will:

Say: We believe in God and that which is revealed to us; and that which was revealed to Ibrahim [Abraham], Isma'il [Ishmael], Ishaq [Isaac], Ya'qub [Jacob] and their descendants; and that which was given to Musa [Moses], 'Isa [Jesus] and other prophets from their Lord. We do not discriminate among any of them, and to God we have surrendered ourselves (in Islam).

(Baqarah 2:136)

However, in addition to the claim of the unity of the Divine, the Qur'anic notion of *tawhid* asserts in unambiguous terms the unity of humanity and the unity of life. Because God's presence transcends human history, so do the values associated with him transcend any particular culture. The message Prophet Muhammad proclaimed was a universal message addressed to humanity and was not limited to the Prophet's ethnic community. The community Prophet Muhammad struggled throughout his life to develop was a moral community. Although Jesus was sent initially to the children of Israel, by the time the Islamic revelation came down, the followers of Christ, the Christians, were already a universal community that embraced ethnic and racial groups from Europe to East Asia, through North and East Africa.

The universality of the final divine message is quite evident throughout the Qur'an. The Qur'an begins with Surah Fatihah ("opening chapter") and concludes with Surah Nas ("humanity chapter"). The first verse of the first chapter of the Qur'an proclaims God as the Lord of all humanity: "all praise is to God the Lord of the worlds." The last verse, similarly, concludes with the word "humanity." Indeed, the Qur'an describes the mission of Prophet Muhammad as one of mercy and compassion to humanity:

We have sent you but, as a mercy to humanity (lil'alamin).

(Anbiya' 21:107)

COMPLETION OF PROPHETS AND MIRACLES

The Seal of Prophets, Prophet Muhammad, was the only prophet who received a clearly and conspicuously universal message, and he was the only prophet who was not supported by miracles to certify the authenticity of his mission. He was asked to proclaim, in response to the repeated demands of his community for miracles, that he was simply a human prophet:

> They say: We shall not believe in you, until you cause a spring to gush forth for us from the earth, or (until) you have a garden of date trees and vines, and cause rivers to gush forth in their midst, carrying abundant water; or you cause the sky to fall in pieces, as you say (will happen), against us; or you bring God and the angels before (us) face to face; or you have a house adorned with gold, or you mount a ladder right into the skies. No, we shall not even believe in your mounting until you send down to us a book that we can read. Say: Glory to my Lord! Am I aught but a human messenger?
>
> (Isra' 17:90–93)

The reason for withholding miracles from the final prophet, the Qur'an points out, was that these miracles were never a reason for people to believe. Early prophets, including Moses and Jesus, were challenged despite delivering supernatural miracles:

> And we refrain from sending the signs, only because the men of former generations treated them as false: we sent the she-camel to the Thamud to open their eyes, but they treated her wrongfully: we only sent the signs by way of warning.
>
> (Isra' 17:59)

The miracle Prophet Muhammad brought, it was pointed out, was the very Qur'an he tirelessly recited to all who were interested in listening to the revealed word.

> If there were a *qur-an* (a book of recitation) with which mountains were moved, or the earth were cloven asunder, or the dead were made to speak, (this would be the Qur'an!) but, truly, the command is with God in all things! Do not the believers know that, had God (so) willed, he could have guided all mankind (to the right)? But the unbelievers, never will disaster cease to seize them for their (ill) deeds, or to settle close to their homes, until the promise of God come to pass, for, verily, God will not fail in his promise.
>
> (Ra'd 13:31)

The miracles human beings needed to see were all around them in God's creation. There are plenty of signs in the universe that continuously point towards the greatness and majesty of the creator:

> Among his signs is this: that he created you from dust; and then, behold, you are people scattered (far and wide)! And among his signs is this: that he created for you mates from among yourselves, that you may dwell in tranquility with them, and he has put love and mercy between your (hearts): verily in that are signs for those who reflect. And among his signs is the creation of the heavens and the earth, and the variations in your languages and your colors; verily in that are signs for those who know. And among his signs is the sleep that you take by night and by day, and the quest that you (make for livelihood) out of his bounty: verily in that are signs for those who hearken.

And among his signs, he shows you the lightning, by way both of fear and of hope, and he sends down rain from the sky and with it gives life to the earth after it is dead: verily in that are signs for those who are wise. And among his signs is this: that heaven and earth stand by his command; then when he calls you, by a single call, from the earth, behold, you (straightway) come forth.

(Rum 30:20–25)

Prophet Muhammad's mission signaled the end of the age of miracles and the beginning of the age of reason. Discovering the truth and returning to the original Spirit no more requires sending new messengers supported with miracles. It rather requires the struggle of sensible and authentic persons with great passion to reclaim the transcendental truth and guidance.

CHAPTER 4

Engaging Religiosity

The religious is often juxtaposed to the secular, but this is by no means the only dichotomy relevant to religious life today. Another equally important juxtaposition is between the religious and the spiritual. A third one is between the religious and the cultural. The fact that people often need to juxtapose religion with society, spirituality, and culture points to the affinity they all have to one another.

However, before we delve to explore the relationship between religion and the other three realms of human experience, a quick delineation of the Qur'anic usage of the term "religion" (or "*din*," in Arabic) is in order.

The word *din* connotes both the ideas of judgment and indebtedness. The Qur'an, for instance, uses the word "*din*" in Surah Yusuf (Yusuf 12:67) in reference to the legal convention of the old Egyptians which required the enslavement of a thief by the owner of the stolen object, a convention that Prophet Yusuf (Joseph) employed to take custody of his brother Benjamin. Similarly, the Qur'an refers to the day of judgment as the day of *din*. In broader sense, the term "religion" is used in the Qur'an in reference to the set of values and beliefs revealed to humanity through the agency of prophets:

> Behold! God took the covenant of the prophets, saying: I give you a book and wisdom; then comes to you a messenger, confirming what is with you; do you believe him and render him help. God said: Do you agree, and take this my covenant as binding on you? They said: We agree. He said: Then bear witness, and I am with you among the witnesses. If any turn back after this, they are perverted transgressors. Do they seek for other than the religion (*din*) of God? While all creatures in heavens and on earth have, willingly or unwillingly, bowed to his will (accepted Islam), and to him shall they all be brought back.
>
> (Al 'Imran 3:81–83)

"Religion" in the above verses is used in reference to the obligations
the faithful incur as result of the covenant they make with God when they
accept divine revelation. In calling humanity to observe its religious obligations toward the Divine, the Qur'an asserts that these obligations are
not intended as a set of demands that require self-denial or withdrawing
from an engaging and assertive life here and now, but as one that recon-
ciles individual and collective life. A true religion is in synchrony with
the innate human nature:

> So set your face steadily and truly to the faith (*din*): (establish) God's handi-
> work according to the pattern on which he has made mankind: no change
> (let there be) in the work (wrought) by God: that is the true religion (*din*):
> but most among mankind understand not.
>
> (Rum 30:30)

SERVING GOD BY SERVING HUMANITY

In most known religious traditions, religious devotion requires one to
withdraw from life and to deny oneself— to shun self-fulfilling and self-
rewarding endeavors and to avoid all that brings pleasure and satisfaction. The religious person par excellence in most religions is the monk:
the person who rejects earthly activities and devotes himself to a life of
inner contemplation and remembrance of the Divine.

The Qur'an rejects the model of the monk as the way to attain the highest form of religiosity, as it rejects the claim that this form of seeking a true
life was ordained by God:

> But the monasticism which they invented for themselves, we did not pre-
> scribe to them: (we commanded) only that they seek the pleasure of God.
> But that they did not foster as they should have done.
>
> (Hadid 57:27)

The Qur'an, on the other hand, sees religiosity—that is, a life devoted
to the pleasure of God—as an act of positive engagement in the world.
Islam teaches that to be religious is to assert oneself, to be in the world,
to act and to do, to positively impact one's surroundings and to make a
difference in the life of one's family, community, and the larger society—
in short, to be the moral agent (*khalifah*) of the Divine.

It is for this reason that the Qur'an praises those who are active in the
world, busying themselves in doing what is good, right, and just. The
Qur'an praises those who give out of their wealth, help those in need,
build public facilities that enhance human life, teach and educate, enjoin
the right and forbid evil, and strive with their possessions and persons
in the way of God.

To be religious is to be devout, but devotion to God does not culminate
in worshiping the Divine, but in serving humanity. Acts of devotion, such

as prayers, rekindle the human spirit with divine inspiration, but devotion to God must manifest itself in acts of charity and goodness towards other human beings.

Being religious is not intended to give a particular reward or benefit to God. God has made it clear that Qur'anic guidance is meant to make people better human beings and more true to their *fitra* (human nature). It is meant to make people's lives more rewarding and their community governed by the principles of goodness and justice. In Chapter Hujurat the Qur'an addresses this very issue in the most eloquent way:

> They impress on you as a favor that they have embraced Islam. Say: Count not your Islam as a favor upon me: nay, God has conferred a favor on you that he has guided you to the faith, if you are true and sincere.
>
> (Hujurat 49:17)

> If the people of the towns had but believed and feared God, we should indeed have opened out to them (all kind of) blessings, from heaven and earth; but they rejected the truth, and we brought them to book for their misdeeds.
>
> (A'raf 7:96)

By the same token, defying the will of God and rejecting faith brings no harm to God, nor does it do him injustice, but it indeed brings harm to those who reject a truthful life. In commenting on the disobedience of those who refused to abide by the commandments of God, the Qur'an states: "To us they did no harm but they harmed their own souls" (Baqarah 2:57).

The interconnectedness between serving God and serving humanity, and between promoting divine purpose and advancing social life, is unmistakable to anyone who is familiar with the Qur'anic message. The Qur'an declares that promoting equity and justice in human society is the reason for sending messengers and revealing books: "We sent our messengers with clear signs and sent down with them the book and the balance (of right and wrong) that humans may stand forth in justice" (Hadid 57:25).

The Qur'an also stresses that the enduring legacy people can leave behind is related to actions that were intended for the benefit of humanity. All else is bound to dissipate and disappear: "For the scum disappears like froth cast out; while that which is for the good of humankind remains on the earth" (Ra'd 13:17).

Serving humanity as the way to serving God is particularly clear in the Islamic revelation that was meant to be the last divine revelation. The mission of Prophet Muhammad, that God's blessing and mercy may surround him, is described as that of "mercy to humanity." Muslims who carry the legacy of the last prophet are duty bound to maintain it through their actions and interactions. The challenge facing today's

Muslims is to carry out the prophetic legacy and to show compassion beyond their own families and communities. Unless and until the Muslim communities exemplify the principle of "mercy to humanity," they need to reevaluate the extent to which they are devoted to God.

DEVOTION, NOT AFFILIATION

Attaining high religiosity is directly linked to human intention and action. Attaining God's blessings is not a matter of being affiliated with a religious community, or being born into a particular religion. Rather, the Qur'an associates faith with good work and good deeds. It is through positive action that people assert their religiosity.

> Not your wishes, nor those of the People of the Book (can prevail); whoever works evil will be requited accordingly. Nor will he find besides God any protector or helper.
>
> (Nisa' 4:123)

Similarly the Qur'an links the triumph of good over evil, and the triumph of faith over corruption, to the struggle of the faithful:

> If it had been God's will, he could certainly have exacted retribution from them. But (he lets you struggle) in order to test you, some with others.
>
> (Muhammad 47:4)

This does not mean that the Qur'an pays no attention to religious solidarity. The Qur'an indeed stresses the importance of social solidarity among like-minded individuals for translating moral commitments into social practices and institutions, and it thus urges believers to cooperate with other believers who share with them their moral commitments and values.

> The unbelievers are protectors, one of another: unless you do this, (protect each other), there would be tumult and oppression on earth, and great mischief.
>
> (Anfal 8:73)

Yet this solidarity is not absolute but must always be subjected to the transcendental principles of goodness and justice. Such a condition safeguards against efforts by egoistic and unscrupulous leaders to harness religious devotion for advancing narrow interests.

The religious identity the Qur'an promotes is an engaging religiosity that requires the believer to take active part in social life, and to translate his or her love and commitment to God into positive and caring attitudes toward God's creation. This is a religiosity that helps the believer transcend parochial interests and concerns, and work constantly for improving the human condition and uplifting the human spirit.

CHAPTER 5

Trust in God

Human life exhibits two contradictory qualities: vulnerability and invincibility. Human life is very fragile. Individual life can be easily, or so it seems, terminated by determined enemies, yet still the individual can challenge effectively the most powerful social and political orders. Human history is saturated with stories of individuals who were abused, enslaved, or murdered. It sometimes takes only a moment of anger, recklessness, or overwhelming greed to finish a vibrant individual life. Yet history is replete with individuals whose visionary and courageous acts changed the direction of their communities, even the direction of human history.

What makes an individual a victim or a hero is a complex question, but an important element in the equation of victimization and heroism is the relationship between the human will and the divine will. It is in the convergence of the human and divine wills that we do find human greatness. It is in responding positively and genuinely to the divine will that triumphant lives can be made. The Qur'an uses the term *"tawakkul,"* or *"trust,"* to signify such convergence.

The convergence of the divine and the human will also forms the boundary where the human spirit recognizes its divine origin through faith. Trust in God is the line that links spirit with faith. For trusting God is nothing other than trusting one's own spirit. After all, a person would be able to respond to the divine will and command only when he or she is able to respond to the inner voice that calls to embrace truth and to privilege justice.

SPIRIT AND EGO

The human spirit belongs to the world of transcendence, while ego is of the natural world. Both are intrinsic to human life. The human spirit embodies the divine voice because it emanates directly from the divine spirit and yearns to return to it. The human spirit hides within it that voice that urges us to do the right thing and maintain justice and balance. This hidden voice is what modern psychology constantly refers to as our "conscience."

The ego, on the other hand, belongs to the natural order and focuses on immediate desires and needs. It is the voice of the self-centered individuality that urges us to pursue our self-interests unfettered, and it places individual inclinations over all other considerations, including moral considerations—that is, the consideration of the rights and dignity of other individuals. It is therefore by remembering God and being conscious of his will and presence that the spirit can balance the ego. Recognizing the priority of the divine will over the human, and subordinating individual interests and needs to the demands of truth and justice, is the essence of human spirituality. Such recognition is the true mark of having profound trust in divine goodness and justice, as well as the manifestation of *"tawakkul,"* that is, placing one's trust in God.

> And for those who fear God, he (ever) prepares a way out, and he provides for them from (sources) they never could imagine. And if anyone puts his trust in God, sufficient is (God) for him. For God will surely accomplish his purpose: verily, for all things has God appointed a due proportion.
>
> (Talaq 65:2–3)

The above verse relates the believer's consciousness of God to his ability to place his trust in the Divine, asserting that these qualities result in bringing divine aid and support to the person who possesses them. The sooner the individual aligns himself with the Divine and surrenders his will to him, the sooner God elevates the stature of the faithful and blesses his life. The Qur'anic statement concludes with an important clue: happenings that transpire in an individual's life fall within a greater scheme of things, a scheme that corresponds with divine purpose. And so a complete belief in the goodness of the sublime values demanded by the Divine, along with the willingness to live them out in daily experience, is a question of deep faith. Trusting God is not simply an affirmation of one's faith, but it is also the acceptance of one's fate—that is, acceptance of the challenges and opportunities that are linked with one's moral and social commitments.

TRUST IS THE MANIFESTATION OF DEEP FAITH

A person who is capable of *tawakkul* is one who has a profound understanding of God's qualities and purposes, as well as profound comprehension of the human condition. That is to say that a person of *tawakkul* is a person of reflection and contemplation, one who recognizes that God's qualities and purposes are relevant to human struggle, and that nothing happens except with the knowledge and permission of God. *Tawakkul* is, therefore, a sign of deep faith in God's wisdom, knowledge, power, mercy, and might—a faith that leads the faithful to realize that true goodness and salvation lie in embracing God's will and plan for humanity.

> If indeed you ask them who it is that created the heavens and the earth, they would be sure to say, God. Say: See you then the things that you invoke besides God; can they, if God wills some penalty for me, remove his penalty? Or if he wills some grace for me, can they keep back his grace? Say: Sufficient is God for me! In him trust those who put their trust.
>
> (Zumar 39:38)

A person of *tawakkul* knows well the human condition and is always aware of human mortality and finitude. He is keenly aware that he is an agent of the immortal and infinite, and that he must therefore face his human condition with courage, determination, hope, and, yes, with resignation to divine knowledge and power. This was the stance of all prophets who were faced with great challenges but always maintained unshaken trust in God:

> Relate to them the story of Nuh [Noah]. Behold! He said to his people: O my People! If it be hard on your (mind) that I should stay (with you) and commemorate the signs of God, yet I put my trust in God. Get you then an agreement about your plan and among your partners, so your plan be not to you dark and dubious. Then pass your sentence on me, and give me no respite.
>
> (Yunus 10:71)

Noah was aware of the threat posed by his people, but he was equally aware of the power and mercy of God, and the imperative to choose the divine principle over human whims. He chose to trust God and do what was right, despite the risk, as he recognized that the risk could not be avoided without succumbing to his natural instincts—privileging the natural over the spiritual and human folly over divine wisdom. So he chose to follow his spiritual instincts and to follow divine commandment, knowing fully that his salvation lay in choosing God.

TRUST IS NOT COMPLACENCY

Trusting God is not, however, a matter of complacency and inaction, but a matter of devotion, commitment, and perseverance. Trusting God means that the human being embraces the universal principles of rightness and justice, develops the plans necessary to pursuing objectives and interests compatible with those principles, and remains steadfast in the face of adversity and resistance.

Trusting God does not mean, however, that one can abdicate his responsibilities and expect God to take care of the things that he neglects to care for, out of laziness or greed. Thus God refuted the leaders of Quraysh who did not want to share their wealth with the less-privileged members of the community, arguing that if God so willed he would have done it himself:

> And when they are told: Spend of the bounties with which God has provided you, the unbelievers say to those who believe: Shall we then feed those whom, if God had so willed, he would have fed, (himself)? You are in nothing but manifest error.
>
> (Yasin 36:47)

The above interesting argument reveals a perverted mind willing to abdicate moral responsibilities toward the less fortunate by blaming poverty and social injustice on God. God is capable of providing for the less fortunate himself, but he did not. So why should we, their argument goes, be asked to cater to the needs of the poor?

What the above argument leaves out is the fact that God has appointed the human being as the moral agent of the Divine, and he has given humans resources and capabilities to control their natural and social environments. Blaming God for the failure of the wealthy and powerful to take responsibility is a cop-out and a blatant abdication of responsibility.

The above example provides an extreme case of complacency that involves assigning blame to God. Yet complacency often takes other, often more-benign forms. Complacency often involves an expectation of divine intervention to correct decadent social conditions. It can be seen, for example, in the refusal of the children of Israel to respond to Moses's call to enter the Holy Land for fear of the risk involved:

> They said: O Musa! While they remain there, never shall we be able to enter, to the end of time. Go and your Lord and fight you two, while we sit here (and watch).
>
> (Ma'idah 5:24)

Taking responsibility for one's condition and situation is essential, and working with great optimism despite mounting difficulties is an act of faith that exemplifies strong trust in God. However, abdicating responsibility under the pretense of reliance on God is complacency that the believer should always be wary of.

This meaning was beautifully captured in a *hadith* reported by Tirmidhi, in which a Bedouin came to the Prophet asking whether he should tie his camel when he was away from it, or should leave it loose and put his trust in God. The Prophet responded: "Tie it and put your trust in God."

PART II

FAITH

Human spirit draws its flame from its divine origin and can keep the flame alive by constantly reconnecting with that divine source. The desire and will to remain faithful to one's source is the essence of the act of faith. Faith is a choice, and all acts of faith are the manifestation of the will to remain true to God.

Faith is a human passion that can have positive impact, both by being enlightened by divine knowledge and by developing a moral vision capable of transforming the world in a positive way. Enlightened knowledge broadens and sharpens faith, and persistence in the face of trying challenges strengthens the faithful.

Faith in its simplest form is the acknowledgement by the human being of the priority of God. It is an act of recognition of the transient nature of the human spirit and of the eternity of the Divine. Faith is an expression of the desire to make peace with God, as well as a clear recognition that a lasting peace must start with bringing harmony between man and God. Faith is an expression of the human longing for eternal peace, and it is the first step toward achieving inner peace, without which social, universal, and eternal peace are untenable.

CHAPTER 6

Revealed Guidance

The Qur'an introduces itself as a book of guidance to those who seek the truth (Baqarah 2:2). Truth envelops matters that are beyond the immediate reach of human beings, and it can be accessed by either of two means: revelation or inspiration.

Truth is anchored in the beyond, the unseen (*ghayb*). The overall meaning of life and existence is not accessible to human senses, because it lies beyond the immediate consciousness of any human being. Issues relating to the beginning and the end, and to the innermost and the outermost of existence, are not open to empirical verification. Human beings are unable to physically observe the beginning or the end of creation, they cannot physically see or hear the Divine, and they cannot physically ascertain afterlife and human destiny. The only immediate access to truth is spiritual, through inspiration or revelation.

While the ultimate truth is beyond the immediate consciousness of humans, it constitutes the core of human existence. Truth lies in the human spirit. The infinite spirit of the Divine is the source of the finite human spirit, and hence the journey to God starts deep within the human soul. The journey to God is a spiritual journey that starts with a decisive choice to seek the truth. Choosing God over and above all else is the first act of faith that marks the spiritual awakening of the human being.

People are inspired to seek God and the values and principles associated with him by their very human spirit. The human spirit is inspired by its innate nature to seek goodness, rightness, justice, and compassion. However, when social practices become corrupt, human nature is also corrupted, as society socializes new generations to engage in corrupt practices. Under such circumstances, the human spirit is no more inspired to seek the truth, and it can only be saved from its state of corruption through revelation that aims at awakening the innate nature of humanity.

Prophet Noah experienced one of the most extreme conditions of corruption, as he came slowly to the sad conclusion that the community to which he devoted his extraordinarily long life was beyond redemption and doomed to perpetuate the state of rampant corruption:

> And Noah said: O my Lord! Leave not of the unbelievers, a single one on earth! For, if you do leave (any of) them, they will but mislead your servants, and they will breed none but wicked ungrateful ones.
>
> (Nuh 71:26)

When the inner voice that inspires people to seek the truth is silenced, God reveals the truth to prophets, in order to guide humanity out of the darkness of ignorance and corruption to the light of truth and justice:

> ...a book which we have revealed unto you in order that you might lead mankind out of the depths of darkness into light—by the leave of their Lord—to the way of the exalted in power, worthy of all praise!
>
> (Ibrahim 14:1)

> And thus have we, by our command, sent inspiration to you: you knew not (before) what the revealed book was, and what faith was; but we have made the (Qur'an) a light, wherewith we guide such of our servants as we will; and verily you do guide to the straight way.
>
> (Shura 42:52)

BOOK OF GUIDANCE

The guidance God revealed to humanity through the agency of prophets was given in the form of the scripture, a revealed message that was committed to a written word. Divine revelation is received today in the form of a book accessible to all those who are capable of reading. Indeed, the Qur'an uses the term "book" to refer to all the revelations that were sent by God to prophets, and it uses the term "the People of the Book" to refer to the followers of divine revelations. The Qur'an asserts that it is the seal of all divine revelation, and that it confirms the essential divine message embodied in all of them:

> And this is a book which we have sent down, bringing blessings, and confirming (the revelations) which came before it.
>
> (An'am 6:92)

The book, or *alkitab* in Arabic, is derived from the root "*kataba*," which means "to write." The word is also used in the Qur'an to mean "prescribe." The Qur'an, for instance, states that God has prescribed (*kataba*) mercy on himself. The Qur'an also uses the word "book" to refer to the deliberate design of God's creation.

> With him are the keys of the unseen, the treasures that none knows but he. He knows whatever there is on the earth and in the sea. Not a leaf does fall

but with his knowledge: there is not a grain in the darkness (or depths) of the earth, nor anything fresh or dry (green or withered), but is (inscribed) in a record clear (to those who can read).

(An'am 6:56)

The Qur'an uses the term "book" to refer to the way the divine will is manifested in both nature and history. The natural order is the way it is because it reflects God's will and design, and the social order is the way it is because it responds to God's order and command. God's will manifests itself in the natural order of the elaborate universe that exhibits a high level of regularity and internal consistency, which forms the book of creation. Similarly, God's will manifests itself in human history, through human actions of individuals committed to the values and principles revealed in the book of guidance. The free acts of human beings in support of or opposition to divine guidance are, however, constrained by another book, the book of historical necessity.

No misfortune can happen on earth or in your souls but is recorded in a decree before we bring it into existence: that is truly easy for God: in order that you may not despair over matters that pass you by, nor exult over favors bestowed upon you. For God loves not any vainglorious boaster.

(Hadid 57:22–23)

The above verse stresses that nothing happens in society but in accordance with an unfolding divine plan, one which necessitates that truth must overcome falsehood, justice must triumph over injustice, and good must outwit evil. This does not mean that human beings do not have the free will to choose falsehood, injustice, or evil, but that in the interplay between good and evil, the latter is bound to collapse under its own weight and to be undermined by the very forces that promote it.

The book of guidance, divine revelation, is therefore essential to help human beings establish a social order compatible with both history and creation. The guidance embodied in the book is only open to those who are ready to overcome their personal and immediate needs and seek the truth with open minds and hearts:

Verily this Qur'an does guide to that which is most right (or stable), and gives the glad tidings to the believers who work deeds of righteousness, that they shall have a magnificent reward.

(Isra' 17:9)

However, when the ego is elevated above God, the mind is closed and the heart is hardened; truth becomes elusive and inaccessible:

We have explained (things) in various (ways) in this Qur'an, in order that they may receive admonition, but it only increases their flight (from the truth)!

(Isra' 17:41)

And we put coverings over their hearts (and minds) lest they should understand the Qur'an, and deafness into their ears: when you do remember your
Lord and him alone in the Qur'an, they turn on their backs, fleeing (from the
truth).

(Isra' 17:46)

ETERNAL MIRACLE AND FINAL REVELATION

All prophets sent by God to guide humanity were supported with
miracles to help them validate their divine authority, except Prophet
Muhammad. The only miracle Prophet Muhammad received was the
Qur'an.

If there were a qur'an (a book of reading) with which mountains were
moved, or the earth were cloven asunder, or the dead were made to speak,
(this would be this Qur'an!) it, truly, the command is with God in all things!
Do not the believers know, that, had God (so) willed, he could have guided
all mankind (to the right)?

(Ra'd 13:31)

Had we sent down this Qur'an on a mountain, verily, you would have seen it
humble itself and cleave asunder for fear of God. Such is the similitude
which we propound to men that they may reflect.

(Hashr 59:21)

Say: If the whole of mankind and *jinns* were to gather together to produce the
like of this Qur'an, they could not produce the like thereof, even if they
backed up each other with help and support.

(Isra' 17:88)

The miracle of the Qur'an is not limited to its stylistics, which challenged the pre-Islamic Arab society that prided itself in its ability to mold
the language into the most elegant poetic expressions. The Qur'an also
challenges those who doubt its authenticity by pointing to its internal
and external consistency.

And no question do they bring to you but we reveal to you the truth and the
best explanation (thereof).

(Furqan 25:33)

Do they not consider the Qur'an (with care)? Had it been from other than
God, they would surely have found therein much discrepancy.

(Nisa' 4:82)

Yet the extraordinary power of the Qur'an is always felt by those who
read it with an open heart and mind. Those who come to it with a sincere
desire to find the truth will find in the Qur'an guidance, healing, and
tranquility, while those who are not ready to place truth over and above
their little egos will be turned off by its sublime message:

We send down (stage by stage) in the Qur'an that which is a healing and a
mercy to those who believe: to the unjust it causes nothing but loss after loss.

(Isra' 17:82)

The Qur'an has a unique style. It speaks to the human soul in its
entirety, to both its intellectual and emotional elements. It uses a concrete
language to convey the most abstract meaning, thereby speaking to both
intellectuals and lay persons. And unlike regular books that are organized
thematically to elaborate particular points, the Qur'an presents its sub-
jects in a manner that forces the reader to pause and reflect on the meaning delivered. It returns to issues it discusses frequently, in order to
elaborate on different aspects and bring new insights into a topic that it
discussed earlier. Muslim exegesists endeavored to uncover the overall
themes that run through the various verses that constitute the different
chapters of the Qur'an. Still, Qur'anic themes run across various chapters,
requiring readers who want to identify Qur'anic views on a particular
theme to relate and contrast all the Qur'anic verses relevant to the issue
at hand.

READING THE QUR'AN

Frequent and repeated reading of the Qur'an helps the reader to
develop a Qur'anic worldview and a deep sense of the Qur'anic message.
Articulating the Qur'anic meaning requires, however, more systematic
and consistent approach. To begin with, the Qur'an requires its readers
to understand those verses that have nuanced meaning in the light of
the self-evident verses:

He it is who has sent down to you the book: in it are verses with clear and
established meaning; they are the foundation of the book: others have
nuanced meaning. But those in whose hearts is perversity follow the part
thereof that is nuanced, seeking discord, and searching for its hidden
meanings, but no one knows its hidden meanings except God. And those
who are firmly grounded in knowledge say: We believe in the book; the
whole of it is from our Lord: and none will grasp the message except men
of understanding.

(Al 'Imran 3:7)

In the absence of a systematic approach to understanding the Qur'an,
readers with ulterior motives would succeed in distorting the message.
This is usually done by selectively focusing on certain verses of the
Qur'an, while overlooking others that bring an additional insight that
would compel the interpreter to balance out one verse by means of
another.

The Qur'an is, therefore, critical of all fragmented reading of the
revealed text, for such reading is bound to distort the intended message

of revelation. In fact, it may underscore an ill will on the part of those who cherry-pick Qur'anic verses to support a particular viewpoint that would not otherwise be supported by the Qur'anic text.

> Then is it only a part of the book that you believe in, and do you reject the rest? But what is the reward for those among you who behave like this but disgrace in this life? On the day of judgment they shall be consigned to the most grievous penalty. For God is not unmindful of what you do.
>
> (Baqarah 2:85)

Reading out of context is a long-standing problem in the history of interaction between people and the revealed word, the modern equivalent of which is the problem of quoting out of context. Both Muslim extremists and those who blame their extremism on the Qur'an employ a selective approach to reading the Qur'anic text, thus both are guilty of misrepresenting the Qur'anic message. The Qur'anic teachings in the area of peace and war are a case in point. The extremists pretend that the Qur'an exhorts believers to wage war against unbelievers by citing the following verses:

> O Prophet! Strive hard against the unbelievers and the hypocrites, and be firm against them. Their abode is hell, an evil refuge indeed.
>
> (Tawbah 9:73)

> When you meet the unbelievers in the battlefield, strike off their heads and, when you have laid them low, bind your captives firmly.
>
> (Muhammad 47:4)

> O you who believe! Fight the unbelievers who gird you about, and let them find firmness in you: and know that God is with those who fear him.
>
> (Tawbah 9:123)

The extremists misrepresent Islam by arguing that the Qur'an directs Muslims to fight non-Muslims on account of having different faith. They do that by obscuring both the textual and historical contexts of the verses they cite. The Qur'an is, however, unequivocal in stressing that fighting is a last resort, only permitted to repulse aggression and stop oppression and abuse: "A declaration of disavowal from God and his messenger to those of the polytheists (Arab pagans) with whom you contracted a mutual alliance" (Tawbah 9:1). The reason for this war against the pagans was their continuous fight and conspiracy against the Muslims to drive them out of Medina as they had been driven out of Makkah. The war also resulted from the pagans' failure to abide by the peace treaty they concluded with the Muslims: "Why you not fight people who violated their oaths, plotted to expel the messenger, and attacked you first" (Tawbah 9:13).

Among the many Qur'anic verses left out of the extremist discussion are those that direct Muslims to initiate fighting only to repel aggression, while urging them to seek peace when the other party seeks peace:

Fight in the way of God those who fight you, but do not commit aggression, for God loves not aggressors. And fight them wherever you meet them, and turn them out from where they have turned you out; for persecution is worse than slaughter. But if they cease, God is oft-forgiving, most merciful. And fight them on until there is no oppression and the religion is only for God, but if they cease, let there be no hostility except to those who practice oppression.

(Baqarah 2:190–193)

The right approach to reading the Qur'an does not look at the revealed verses as fragments to be read in isolation of one another, so that a preconceived notion is supported by the Qur'an, but it rather treats them as part of a Qur'anic discourse, such that the meaning of any part of it must be informed by the meaning of the other parts. Such an approach is expected from those who sincerely seek the truth.

Those to whom we have sent the book study it as it should be studied: they are the ones that believe in the book: those who reject faith, the loss is their own.

(Baqarah 2:121)

CHAPTER 7

Knowledge and Wisdom

Knowledge is at the heart of the Islamic faith and forms the basis of Islamic traditions. Knowledge, the Qur'an asserts, is the foundation of strong faith, and the first step in the path to enlightened life. The first divine commandment to the Prophet of Islam was not "believe" or "obey," but "read." It is in the act of reading and in the willingness to keep one's mind open that a true faith is born.

The early biographers of Prophet Muhammad reported his first encounter with Archangel Gabriel, who carried the divine revelation to him. Ibn Hisham narrated that Gabriel approached Muhammad while the latter was asleep in the cave of Hira on the outskirts of the city of Makkah. The angel said to Muhammad, "Read." Muhammad answered in surprise, "I do not know how to read." He felt as if the angel had strangled him and then released him, and he heard once more the command, "Read." Muhammad replied again: "I do not know how to read." Once more he felt the angel strangling and then releasing him, and he heard him repeat the command, "Read." Fearing that the strangling would be stronger, Muhammad answered, "What shall I read?" The angel replied, "Read in the name of your Lord, the Creator, who created man of a clot of blood. Read! Your Lord is most gracious. It is he who taught humans by the pen that which they knew not" ('Alaq 96:1–5).

The command to read preceded the command to believe and to be faithful. This is because knowledge, reflection, and reasoning are the foundation of faith. A true faith is an examined faith, and an examined faith requires the ability to engage in a rational discourse so as to distinguish between truth and falsehood, and between knowledge and fiction.

THE LOCUS OF KNOWLEDGE

The written word, the textbook, is the medium through which knowledge is acquired, developed, examined, ascertained, and transmitted.

Yet knowledge does not reside in the book itself, and its locus is not the text. The locus of knowledge is in the knower, in the person who seeks knowledge, advances knowledge, and nurtures knowledge in society. Knowledge resides in the scholar who strives diligently to receive knowledge from those who came before, to relate it to the human setting in which he or she lives, and to pass it on to others after he adds his own contributions by contributing elements, so to speak, of his own lifetime and experience.

No knowledge without knowers, and no scholarship without scholars—this essential fact has been underscored in an important prophetic statement that stresses in deliberate and unequivocal terms the locus of knowledge. In a *hadith* that was reported by Imam Bukhari and Imam Muslim on the authority of Abdullah bin Amr bin Al-'As, the Prophet said:

> God does not remove knowledge by erasing it from the hearts of people, but removes it by removing scholars. Until a time comes when no scholar is left among the people, and so they follow ignorant leaders, who when asked they give advice without knowledge. They will go astray and lead others astray as well.

The above *hadith* reminds us of a simple fact that is easy to confuse or lose: books accumulated from the past, distributed by publishing houses, and collected in public and personal libraries do not by themselves bring knowledge and enlightenment. Transmitted knowledge must ultimately be borne in enlightened souls that can illuminate the hearts, minds, and souls of others. The scholars and scientists who advance knowledge have a special place in Islamic traditions, and both form the category of *ulama*. The Qur'an privileges knowledge and promises great reward to those who seek knowledge.

> Is one who worships devoutly during the hours of the night prostrating himself or standing (in adoration), who takes heed of the hereafter, and who places his hope in the mercy of his Lord, (like one who does not)? Say: Are those equal, those who know and those who do not know? It is those who are endued with understanding that receive admonition.
>
> (Zumar 39:9)

> God will raise up, to (suitable) ranks (and degrees), those of you who believe and who have been granted knowledge. And God is well-acquainted with all you do.
>
> (Mujadilah 58:11)

The Qur'an further asserts that seeking knowledge brings people closer to God and makes them more appreciative of the greatness of the Divine:

> See you not that God sends down rain from the sky? With it we then bring out produce of various colors. And in the mountains are tracts white and

red, of various shades of color, and black intense in hue. And so amongst men and crawling creatures and cattle, are they of various colors. Those truly fear God, among his servants, who have knowledge: for God is exalted in might, oft-forgiving.

(Fatir 35:27–28)

Seeking knowledge for the sake of God is better than spending time in worship. Reaffirming the importance of knowledge and expanding on the meaning provided in the above verse, the Prophet privileged knowledge over worship. It was reported on the authority of Umamah Albahi, a companion of the Prophet, that when two men were mentioned in the presence of the Prophet, one a scholar and the other a diligent worshiper, he said:

> The preference given to the scholar over the person of tremendous worship is that I have over the least of you, then he recited the verse: Those truly fear God, among his servants, who have knowledge.

(Darami and Tirmidhi)

Indeed the Prophet declared in a *hadith* that was reported by Abu Dawud and Tirmidhi that

> Scholars are the heirs of prophets.

It was the responsibility of prophets among the children of Israel to provide guidance and to lead the efforts of reform in their communities every time people went astray. This responsibility has shifted, the Prophet informed us, to the scholars, with the conclusion of prophethood.

If we truly believe that knowledge cannot thrive in the absence of scholars and scientists, the responsibility for safeguarding knowledge is collective, and the community must develop its own learning institutions to educate its scholars.

REASON BETWEEN COHERENCE AND CORRESPONDENCE

Knowledge in the Qur'an is not merely a body of literature but a process as well. The written text has been, and continues to be, the most important repository of knowledge, yet knowledge lies in the relationship between the written text and the free exercise of human reason. Knowledge derived from observation, reflection, experimentation, or narration is transmitted to others through writing. It is then examined by others, and hence becomes open to confirmation, refutation, or modification. This process applies to empirical knowledge, theoretical knowledge, and even revealed knowledge. The Qur'an promotes an approach to knowledge and learning in which human reason is given prominence. The Qur'an calls upon the believers to use reason (*fu'ad*) to verify the two important sources of information and knowledge: narration (hearing) and observation (seeing).

And pursue not that of which you have no knowledge; for every act of
hearing, or of seeing, or of (intuiting in) the heart (*fu'ad*) will be enquired into
(on the day of reckoning).

(Isra' 17:36)

The term "*fu'ad*" is used in the Qur'an in reference to both the emotional and intellectual elements of the human being, and hence it resembles what modern philosophy calls "human consciousness," or what
modern psychology refers to as "emotional intelligence." The intellectual
aspect of the human spirit that we call "reason" is not completely independent of its emotional aspect, particularly when reasoning is done in
relation with social experiences. Human emotions, such as fear, affinity,
hatred, or love, influence people's reasoning and judgment.

The Qur'an has, therefore, refuted the arguments of those who rejected
revelation on the ground that it contradicts the "truth" that was handed
down to them by their parents and forefathers. The Qur'an challenged
those who rejected revelation to use their rational capacity to compare
the claims of their forefathers against the Qur'anic claims, and it protested that they were following in the footsteps of people who were
misguided and who did things that went against human reason.

When it is said to them: Follow what God has revealed: they say: Nay!
We shall follow the ways of our fathers: what! Even though their fathers were
void of wisdom and guidance!

(Baqarah 2:171)

In addressing errors of perception and narration, the Qur'an frequently appeals to the inner logic of the unbelievers' arguments and
points out contradictions in their claims. The Qur'an thereby demon-
strates that the views and beliefs held by those who blindly follow an
unexamined faith inherited from previous generations are incoherent
and contrary to reason.

Yet they worship, besides God, things for which no authority has been sent
down to them, and of which they have (really) no knowledge: for those that
do wrong there is no helper.

(Hajj 22:71)

But they have no knowledge therein. They follow nothing but conjecture;
and conjecture avails nothing against truth.

(Najm 53:28)

Nay, they charge with falsehood that whose knowledge they cannot compass, even before the elucidation thereof has reached them: thus did those
before them make charges of falsehood: but see what was the end of those
who did wrong!

(Yunus 10:39)

The Qur'an rejects as unfounded claims made by individuals on the basis of conjectures and speculation, without clear evidence that link those claims to reliable and certain knowledge. Certainty of any narration is derived either from its origination in an authoritative source, or from being borne out by actual facts through verification. False narration does not satisfy either of these conditions. A hallmark of an authoritative source is its ability to explain reality in a much-convincing and persuasive manner that compels rational beings to accept it as true and authentic.

Rejecting the revealed narrative on the basis of conjectures by people who are neither able to comprehend it and then refute it, nor capable of proving its incongruity with the real world, is a clear indication, the Qur'an stresses, of ignorance, recklessness, and irresponsibility. The Qur'an's authenticity is confirmed by its ability to explain human reality is a coherent and consistent manner.

> And no question do they bring to you but we reveal to you the truth and the best explanation.
>
> (Furqan 25:33)

Further, the Qur'an frequently asks its readers to open their hearts and minds, and to contemplate the divine signs in the observable world. It also engages in empirical examination of the natural order, for there, the Qur'an stresses, the spiritual order manifest itself. "Say: Travel through the earth and see how God did originate creation; so will God produce a later creation: for God has power over all things" ('Ankabut 29:20).

Although no human being has ever witnessed the moment of creation, it is within the human capacity to discover the process of creation by examining God's creation. Scientific research can help humans figure out phenomena as complex as the creation of heaven, earth, and all the life therein. One area of knowledge is clearly beyond human comprehension—knowledge of the hidden future. The future is the domain of divine knowledge alone. Humans can anticipate and speculate about possible trends, but they cannot predict with certainty what the future will bring. This is particularly so regarding knowledge of the day of resurrection:

> Say: I know not whether the (punishment) which you are promised is near, or whether my Lord will appoint for it a distant term. He (alone) knows the unseen, nor does he make anyone acquainted with his mysteries, Except a messenger whom he has chosen: and then he makes a band of watchers march before him and behind him.
>
> (Jinn 72:25)

> They ask you about the (final) hour, when will be its appointed time? Say: The knowledge thereof is with my Lord (alone): none but he can reveal as to when it will occur. Heavy were its burden through the heavens and the earth. Only, all of a sudden will it come to you. They ask you as if you were eager in search thereof: say: The knowledge thereof is with God (alone), but

most men know not. Say: I have no power over any good or harm to myself
except as God wills. If I had knowledge of the unseen, I should have multi-
plied all good, and no evil should have touched me: I am but a warner, and
a bringer of glad tidings to those who have faith.

(A'raf 7:187–188)

Clearly, the above verses establish in no ambiguous terms that only
God knows when the day of judgment will take place, and that the
Prophet had no ability on his own to know that. Further, the verses assert
that the knowledge of when the day of judgment will take place was
unimportant for the Prophet, as it should be of no concern to other
believers. It will come all of a sudden. What matters, then, is that those
who believe that they will be held accountable for what they have done
with their lives must use the time on earth to promote good and oppose
corruption and evil doing, and ensure that their lives are a positive addition to humanity.

WISDOM

Knowledge of eternal truth, properly understood and related to
human experience, and when internalized and embraced, leads to *hikmah*.

Hikmah, or wisdom, is a special quality that can only bring blessing to
those who possess it.

He grants wisdom to whom he pleases; and he to whom wisdom is granted
receives indeed a benefit overflowing; but none will grasp the message but
men of understanding.

(Baqarah 2:269)

The Qur'an also uses the term "judgment" in reference to wisdom, as
wisdom is manifested in sound judgment and good decisions. Wisdom
as sound judgment was given to Prophet Yahya (John) at an early age:

O Yahya! Take hold of the book with might: and we gave him wisdom even
as a youth.

(Maryam 19:12)

As such, wisdom is those elements of knowledge and learning that
inspire good judgment, and hence good choices and actions. The Qur'an
provides examples of wisdom in Surah Isra'.

These are among the (precepts of) wisdom, which your Lord has revealed to
you. Take not, with God, another object of worship, lest you should be
thrown into hell, blameworthy and rejected.

(Isra' 17:39)

The above verse concludes a long list of instances of wisdom
expounded in the Qur'an in the opening verses of Surah Isra'. These
include:

And render to the kindred their due rights, as (also) to those in want, and to the wayfarer: but squander not (your wealth) in the manner of a spendthrift. Verily spendthrifts are brothers of the evil ones; and the evil one is to his Lord (himself) ungrateful. And even if you have to turn away from them in pursuit of the mercy from your Lord which you do expect, yet speak to them a word of easy kindness. Make not your hand tied (like a niggard's) to your neck, nor stretch it forth to its utmost reach, so that you become blameworthy and destitute. Verily your Lord does provide sustenance in abundance for whoever he pleases, and he provides in a just measure: for he does know and regard all his servants. Kill not your children for fear of want: we shall provide sustenance for them as well as for you. Verily the killing of them is a great sin. Nor come nigh to adultery: for it is a shameful (deed) and an evil, opening the road (to other evils). Nor take life—which God has made sacred—except for just cause. And if anyone is slain wrongfully, we have given his heir authority (to demand *qisas* [retribution] or to forgive): but let him not exceed bounds in the matter of taking life; for he is helped (by the law). Come not nigh to the orphan's property except to improve it, until he attains the age of full strength; and fulfill (every) engagement, for (every) engagement, will be enquired into (on the day of reckoning). Give full measure when you measure, and weigh with a balance that is straight; that is the most fitting and the most advantageous in the final determination. And pursue not that of which you have no knowledge; for every act of hearing, or of seeing, or of (feeling in) the heart will be enquired into (on the day of reckoning). Nor walk on the earth with insolence: for you can not rend the earth asunder, nor reach the mountains in height. Of all such things the evil is hateful in the sight of your Lord.

(Isra' 17:26–38)

Wisdom, as portrayed in the above verses, signifies certain attitudes and practices that reflect deep understanding and profound knowledge of what constitutes true, meaningful, and rewarding living. Wisdom is revealed here through the principles that allow individuals to lead a balanced life—principles that include moderation, justice, compassion, integrity, humility, and self-discipline. Wisdom is, therefore, a combination of good learning and good character. A wise person is a person who does not only accumulate knowledge, and understand a great deal about his or her social and natural surrounding, but one who is also capable of translating this knowledge into actions, relations, and institutions. Wisdom is knowledge mixed with courage, consideration, compassion, and just disposition.

Wisdom is the culmination of learning, the combination of knowledge and character, and the manifestation of a wholesome life.

CHAPTER 8

Power of Choice

There is no notion that helps us understand the innate nature of the human being more than the notion of choice. For choice epitomizes the central qualities that set humans apart from other creatures: free will, intelligence, and the capacity to realize freely adopted goals.

The human will, the Qur'an asserts, is free, and humans have the capacity to decide the courses of action they want to pursue. However, with the freedom to pursue one course of action or another, human beings must take full responsibility for the consequences of the actions they make.

> By the soul, and the proportion and order given to it, and its enlightenment as to its wrong and its right; truly he succeeds that purifies it, and he fails that corrupts it!
>
> (Shams 91:7–10)

Human beings have an innate capacity to distinguish right from wrong, and the freedom to pursue either. They have the capacity to choose good or evil with the full understanding of the consequences of both, but they are expected to pursue the good and shun evil. The consequences of pursuing either course of action are not merely external but have internal impact on the overall attitude and inclination of the person: choices are part and parcel of the character formation of the person who undertakes them. For making choices lies at the heart of human experience, and making the right choices that reaffirm our moral obligations is what brings about the moral discipline that we call good character. This is the essence of the process of *tazkiyah* (purification) that the above verse refers to. On the other hand, indulging in wrongdoing, the above verse points out, corrupts people and produces bad character.

ALIGNING HUMAN TO DIVINE WILL

Life is, therefore, a series of choices. Every time we make a choice we engage in an endeavor that defines us and determines our character. The human condition is such that very often the choices that demand more from us are those that help us to be better humans and stronger believers. The power of choice is reflected in many verses of the Qur'an, but verses 175–176 of Surah A'raf make the meaning abundantly clear:

> Relate to them the story of the man to whom we sent our signs, but he passed them by: so Satan followed him up, and he went astray. If it had been our will, we should have elevated him with our signs; but he inclined to the earth, and followed his own vain desires. His similitude is that of a dog: if you pursue him, he lolls out his tongue, or if you leave him alone, he (still) lolls out his tongue. That is the similitude of those who reject our signs; so relate the story perchance they may reflect.
>
> (A'raf 7:175–176)

The Qur'an does not provide further details on the identity of the person it refers to in the above verse, and early Muslim commentators, relying on some biblical accounts, identified him as Balaam the Seer. The biblical story of Balaam suffers from a number of inconsistencies, both as related by the Muslim commentators, and, to a lesser extent, as it is presented in biblical sources, and its reliability has been question.

The meaning of the Qur'anic verse is clear on its own account and is in need of no further external elaboration. The person who is referred to in the above verse made a choice, and his choice was to follow his own self-inclinations rather than the divine will: he was a person who chose his particular interests over and above the universal values revealed to him. Consequently, this person lost his moral compass and lost his inner peace. The parable of the dog is intended to convey the state of mind that characterizes a person who is cut off from divine guidance and is left to his own means—a state of perpetual restlessness.

UNIVERSAL PRINCIPLES OVER SELF-INCLINATIONS

For the human being to fulfill the purpose of human creation, he or she must respond positively to divine revelation and embrace the universal will of the Divine. Unlike the will of transient human beings with limited, emotionally conditioned rationality, the divine will is always universal, aiming at advancing the collective good of humanity.

> O you who believe! Give your response to God and his messenger, when he calls you to that which will give you life; and know that God comes in between a man and his heart, and that it is he to whom you shall (all) be gathered.
>
> (Anfal 8:24)

Responding positively to divine revelation, the Qur'an stresses, empowers both the individual and the community. It empowers the individual by helping him or her to overcome individual limitations as he or she pursues objectives that transcend an individual life. It likewise empowers the collectivity, allowing better cooperation among members of society as they all submit to a transcendental set of principles.

The consequence of rejecting the divine will goes, however, beyond the turmoil and open conflict that result when people place individual good and interests above the common good and the rules of law. The purposeful and intentional rejection of the principles of right and justice would also result in the loss of the moral compass. The Qur'an reaffirms the biblical principle that asserts the priority of moral discipline over material indulgence: "For what is a man profited, if he shall gain the whole world, and lose his own soul?" (Matthew 16:26). As the Qur'an puts it: "By no means! But on their hearts is the stain of the (ill) which they do!" (Mutaffifin 83:14).

The meaning of the verse was clarified by Prophet Muhammad in the tradition that was reported by Tirmidhi and Nasa'i on the authority of Abu Hurayra:

> When a servant of God commits a mistake, a plot of stain appears in his heart, and when he repents his heart clears. However, when he repeats the mistake the stain increases until it eventually covers his entire heart, and this is the staining of the heart.

Insisting on doing evil and indulging in wrongdoing can lead an unrepentant person to lose his or her own soul.

GOOD WILL AND HUMAN INTENTION

Although the Qur'an demands accountability from human beings for the words they utter and deeds they commit freely, it takes, in assessing human culpability, human limitations into account.

> When those come to you who believe in our signs, say: Peace be on you; your Lord has inscribed for himself (the rule of) mercy: verily, if any of you did evil in ignorance, and thereafter repented, and amended (his conduct), lo! He is oft-forgiving, most merciful.
>
> (A'raf 7:54)

Committing an evil act in state of ignorance and weakness should not be a source of desperation, but rather it requires that the faithful repent and renew his or her commitment to the divine principles as soon as he or she becomes aware of the wrongdoing. Repentance is not, however, a calculating act in which a person dispassionately recognizes the evil nature of the wrong done, but rather it must be accompanied by a state of remorse, that is, by an emotional discomfort upon the realization of the awful nature of the evil act. Further, the repentant person must resolve not to repeat the offense, and when the offense is directed against another human being, the person must acknowledge mistakes and compensate for any damage caused by his or her actions.

> God accepts the repentance of those who do evil in ignorance and repent soon afterwards; to them will God turn in mercy: for God is full of knowledge and wisdom. Of no effect is the repentance of those who continue to do evil, until death faces one of them, and he says: Now have I repented indeed; nor of those who die rejecting faith; for them have we prepared a punishment most grievous.
>
> (Nisa' 4:17–18)

Recognizing one's mistakes, and resolving not to repeat them, are effective means for gaining forgiveness. They do not, however, shield a person or a group from the worldly consequences of those actions. Faith and good will are not a substitute for good planning, preparation, and developing the necessary competences and capabilities for achieving the intended goals. Miscalculation by well-meaning individuals does not protect from ill consequences and failure.

> Not your desires, nor those of the People of the Book (can prevail): whoever does wrong, will be requited accordingly. Nor will he find, besides God, any protector or helper.
>
> (Nisa' 4:13)

It took the early Muslims a devastating defeat to learn the hard way that good will and strong faith are not substitutes for good planning and meticulous preparation. The defeat of the Battle of Uhud was overwhelming, resulting in the death of a large number of the Prophet's companions, including Hamza, and it also resulted in the Prophet's injury. The companions wondered how those who rejected faith could triumph over the faithful. The response came swiftly:

> What! When a single disaster smites you, although you smote (your enemies) with one twice as great, do you say? Whence is this? Say: It is from yourselves: for God has power over all things.
>
> (Al 'Imran 3:165)

Yet the Qur'an underscores the fact that while the Prophet's companions must take full responsibility for their failure to win the fight, their defeat happened with the permission of God, as he is in full control over both the universe and human history:

> What you suffered on the day the two armies met was with the leave of God, in order that he might test the believers.
>
> (Al 'Imran 3:166)

God could have intervened, the Qur'an points out, but his will was that he allowed those who rejected faith to win, so that he could test the commitment of the believers and set them apart from those who were lured by the early successes of the faithful:

> If it had been God's will, he could certainly have exacted retribution from them (himself); but (he lets you fight) in order to test you, some with others.
> (Muhammad 47:4)

HUMAN INTENTION AND DIVINE CUNNING

The previous verses from Surah Al 'Imran and Surah Muhammad shed light on the interplay of the divine and human will. Human beings have free will and are able to make their independent choices. They can plan and make necessary preparations in pursuit of particular objectives and goals. But while they have freedom of choice, they cannot be certain that the goals they set out to achieve will be realized.

It is a historical fact that individuals and nations may or may not achieve the goals they intend. Often factors that were not accounted for in the original plans and plots—made by human beings with limited rationality and imperfect knowledge—frustrate the efforts of otherwise quite-capable planners to realize their goals. It is also a historical fact that people may achieve the opposite of what they wanted to achieve in the first place. This is what the Qur'an calls "divine cunning."

One instance of the divine cunning discussed in the Qur'an is the failure of Quraysh, the tribe that opposed Prophet Muhammad, to stop the spread of the Qur'anic message, even though Quraysh spared no effort to frustrate the Prophet and early Muslims, including a failed assassination plot.

> Remember how the unbelievers plotted against you, to keep you in bonds, or slay you, or get you out (of your home). They plot and plan, and God too plans, but the best of planners is God.
>
> (Anfal 8:30)

The Qur'an goes further to assert that evil plotting and planning will always fail, because it is always contrary to the divine will and intention.

> They swore their strongest oaths by God that if a warner came to them, they would follow his guidance better than any (other) of the peoples: but when a warner came to them, it has only increased their flight (from righteousness). On account of their arrogance in the land and their plotting of evil. But the plotting of evil will hem in only the authors thereof. Now are they but looking for the way the ancients were dealt with? But no change will you find in God's way (of dealing): no turning off will you find in God's way (of dealing).
>
> (Fatir 35:42–43)

The inevitable failure of evil plotting is not only due to the fact that it goes against the overall plan of the Divine but also because human beings will always fail to outwit the Divine, as the finite knowledge and rationality of humans will always fall far short in comparison with the infinite knowledge and wisdom of the Divine.

> But you will not, except as God wills: for God is full of knowledge and wisdom.
>
> (Dahr 76:30)

TRUSTING GOD'S DIVINE WISDOM

Given the enormity of the difference between the infinite knowledge and power of the Divine and human limitations, human beings can only grow in wisdom and power when they place their trust in God.

> And if anyone puts his trust in God, sufficient is (God) for him. For God will surely accomplish his purpose: verily, for all things has God appointed a due proportion.
>
> (Talaq 65:3)

Trusting God is not, however, a matter of complacency and inaction, but a matter of devotion, commitment, and perseverance. Trusting God means that the human being embraces the universal principles of rightness and justice, develops the plans necessary to pursuing objectives and interests compatible with those principles, and remains steadfast in the face of challenges and adversities.

CHAPTER 9

Faith and Infidelity

Believing in God and having faith (*iman*) are essential for purposive and meaningful life. Faith brings the human being into harmony with the Divine and brings meaning to the life of the faithful. Faith in the Divine and in the transcendental values associated with him is also essential for establishing the conditions for cooperation among people. Commitment to transcendental values provides a common ground for peoples with varying interests to cooperate in an environment of mutual respect and fair dealing.

DEPTHS OF FAITH

On a closer examination, one can find several levels of meaning of the term "faith" (*iman*). The most basic meaning of faith refers to a person's recognition of certain truths. This recognition can be both intuitive and reasoned. The Qur'an asserts that the recognition of the divine origin of human life is innate to humanity.

> When your Lord drew forth from the children of Adam from their loins, their descendants, and made them testify concerning themselves, (saying): Am I not your Lord (who cherishes and sustains you)? They said: Yea! We do testify! (this), lest you should say on the day of judgment: Of this we were never mindful.

> (A'raf 7:172)

The innate propensity to faith that all human beings share forms the foundation of the deeper sense of faith that the Qur'an encourages. In its basic form, faith manifests itself in the spiritual yearning to the Divine that all humans have, which is often manifested in the sense of spiritual and emotional void people experience when God is kept outside human consciousness. The basic sense of faith is also manifested in the respect and admiration people have for divine qualities, and for those who place moral duties over self-interests and self-inclinations.

People who share the basic sense of faith would still differ greatly in their conception of the Divine and the way he relates to humanity and the universe. Thus the Qur'an presents the struggle of Prophet Ibrahim (Abraham) to find God as an instance of the search for true faith.

> Lo! Ibrahim said to his father Azar: Do you take idols for gods? For I do indeed see that you and your people are in manifest error. So also did we show Ibrahim the power and the laws of the heavens and the earth, that he might (with understanding) have certitude. When the night covered him over, he saw a star and said: This is my lord. But when it set, he said: I love not those that set. When he saw the moon rising in splendor, he said: This is my lord. But when the moon set, he said: Unless my lord guides me, I shall surely be among those who go astray. When he saw the sun rising in splendor, he said: This is my lord; this is the greatest (of all). But when the sun set, he said: O my people! I am indeed free from your (guilt) of giving partners to God. For me, I have set my face, firmly and truly, towards him who created the heavens and the earth, and never shall I give partners to God.
>
> (An'am 6:74–79)

Ibrahim's journey to God took the form of a rational reflection on the universe. He was troubled with the idolatry of his community and recognized that the true Divine cannot reside in human-carved idols, not even in the most majestic and imposing celestial bodies, but must be the source of all.

An informed and examined faith in the Divine is essential, the Qur'an stresses, for developing an inner capacity to respond positively to divine directives and commandments—to submit to the Divine. Thus all verses that call on people to undertake moral or religious duties begin with phrase "O you who believe." For having faith in God is a precondition for serving him and accepting divine guidance.

FAITH BETWEEN RECOGNITION AND COMMITMENT

While faith as recognition of the truth is essential for accepting divine revelation, it may not represent a strong commitment to all aspects of a good and just life. The Qur'an puts the idea in concrete and crisp terms:

> The desert Arabs say: We believe. Say: You have no faith, but you should (only) say, we have submitted our wills to God, for not yet has faith entered your hearts. But if you obey God and his messenger, he will not belittle aught of your deeds: for God is oft-forgiving, most merciful.
>
> (Hujurat 49:14)

The desert Arabs, the Qur'an emphasizes, were lacking in faith. Not that they rejected revelation, for obviously they accepted the basic teachings of Islam. The faith they espoused had no depth to sustain them beyond the general religious practices that signify their submission to the Divine. Faith, the Qur'an makes abundantly clear, has not "entered the hearts" of the desert Arabs in ways that create strong and positive commitment to strive for moral excellence.

Yet the Qur'an does not dismiss this level of acceptance of the revealed truth as insignificant. For every good deed, no matter how little it may be, is regarded as a positive contribution worthy of recognition and reward by God.

Still, the level of faith that deserves the greatest recognition and reward is one that displays deep commitment to the principles of truth, goodness, and justice, as the next verse of the same surah explains:

> Only those are believers who have believed in God and his messenger, and have never since doubted, but have striven with their belongings and their persons in the way of God: such are the sincere ones.
>
> (Hujurat 49:15)

Taking this latter definition of faith as a deep commitment to transcendental truth, those who qualify as faithful are, the Qur'an stresses, few:

> Despite your ardent desire, most human beings are not faithful.
>
> (Yusuf 12:103)

The above verse should not be taken, as some literalist interpretations suggest, to mean that most people do not recognize God, but that most people do not display the level of moral commitment associated with deep faith. The verse must, after all, be understood in the context of Surah Yusuf (Joseph), and in reference to the immoral behavior of Prophet Yusuf's brothers.

The Qur'an frequently uses the term "moral excellence" to signify this depth of faith. Moral excellence, or *ihsan*, is a state of faith that shows high commitment to transcendental values. The meaning of *ihsan* is made clear in *hadith* Jibril (Gabriel) that was reported by Bukhari on the authority of Abu Hurayra:

> A person came to the Prophet and asked him, while we were in his presence: Tell me about faith (*iman*). [The Prophet] said: To believe in God, his angels, his books, his messengers, and fate—both the good and the bad—[occurring with the knowledge and permission] of God. Then [the person] said: Tell me about Islam. [The Prophet] said: The declaration that there is no god but God, establishing prayers, giving charity (*zakah*), fasting Ramadan, and making pilgrimage to the House (*hajj*) by able persons. The [man] said: Then tell me about moral excellence (*ihsan*). [The Prophet] said: To serve God as if you see him, for if you do not see him he sees you. When the man left, the Prophet turned to us and said: Gabriel came to you to teach you your religion.
>
> (Bukhari)

FAITH ACROSS RELIGIONS

It should have become evident by now that "faith" or *"iman"* is a dynamic term that cannot be reduced to the simplistic understanding often associated with the literalist interpretations of the Qur'an. The dynamic nature of Qur'anic terms can also be extended to other terms frequently associated with *"iman"*: infidelity (*"kufr"*) and submission ("Islam").

The tendency to associate faith with members of the Muslim community and deny it to others cannot be supported by a fair and thorough reading of the Qur'an. Jurists who deny faith to non-Muslims cite several verses of the Qur'an that describe followers of Christianity and Judaism as infidels (*kafir*).

> The Jews call 'Uzair (Ezra) a son of God, and the Christians call Al-Masih (Messiah) the son of God. That is a saying from their mouth; (in this) they but imitate what the unbelievers of old used to say. God's disgrace with them: how they are deluded away from the truth!
>
> (Tawbah 9:30)

The term *"katalahum* God," translated here as "God's disgrace," is an old Arabic expression frequently used even among acquaintances to express strong rebuke, which literally means "may God bring death to you." It is a bit stronger expression than another similarly widely-used expression by early Arabs, expressing strong disagreement, *"thakilatka ummuk,"* which literally means "may your mother loose you to death." Both would have been used by close acquaintances who did not intend anything other than expressing displeasure and strong disagreement with a statement or action they just heard or observed. In this context, the Qur'an does not describe the Jews and Christians as infidels, but only as people who emulate the sayings of unbelievers.

In another verse, the Qur'an considers the act of equating God and Jesus as an act of *"kufr"* and deviation from true faith in God:

> They do blaspheme who say: God is Al-Masih [the Messiah] the son of Maryam. But said Al-Masih: O Children of Israel! Worship God, my Lord and your Lord. Whoever joins other gods with God, God will forbid him the garden, and the fire will be his abode. There will for the wrongdoers be no one to help.
>
> (Ma'idah 5:72)

This verse assigns an act of blasphemy to those who say that God is the Messiah, and it warns those who persist in their claims of punishment in the hereafter. But the above two verses should not be taken as a general and all-encompassing statement with regard to all Jews and Christians. For these verses have to be balanced in relation to others that ascribe faith and fidelity to the followers of these two Abrahamic faiths.

And there are, certainly, among the People of the Book, those who believe in God, in the revelation to you, and in the revelation to them, bowing in humility to God: they will not sell the signs of God for a miserable gain! For them is a reward with their Lord, and God is swift in account.

(Al 'Imran 3:199)

Similarly, the Qur'an repeatedly insists that salvation is not exclusively the lot of the follower of the final revelation but is also open to the followers of other religious traditions. The criteria the Qur'an establishes for reward is not affiliation with any particular religion, but true devotion to divine truth and guidance.

Those who believe (in the Qur'an), those who follow the Jewish (scriptures), the Christians and the Sabians—any who believe in God and the last day, and work righteousness—on them shall be no fear, nor shall they grieve.

(Ma'idah 5:69)

RECOGNITION BETWEEN FAITH AND INFIDELITY

As recognizing the Divine is a precondition for accepting divine revelation, so does deep faith prompt the faithful to lead a truthful and sincere life. The Qur'an repeatedly urges the faithful to submit fully to justice and goodness.

O you who believe! Fear God as he should be feared, and die not except in a state of submission (Islam).

(Al 'Imran 3:102)

The state of being that the Qur'an calls people to realize is a state of submission to divine guidance—not merely service and worship, but it is equally that of manifesting true faith through good deeds. The state of Islam, being, as the Qur'an describes it, the state of sincere devotion to God, is therefore the desired state of being:

The religion before God is Islam (submission to his will): nor did the People of the Book dissent therefrom except through envy of each other, after knowledge had come to them. But if any deny the signs of God, God is swift in calling to account.

(Al 'Imran 3:19)

The above meaning is reiterated in the statement of Prophet Muhammad, who stressed that submission to divine will, and following divine guidance, is the true sign of faith.

None of you is truly a believer until his inclinations are brought in line with what I have brought.

(Tabarani)

Yet the relationship between faith and infidelity, or *iman* and *kufr,* is not simple or straightforward when it comes to social expression and

personal confession. For here, as the Qur'an expounds on this complex
relationship in great detail, the relationship is exceedingly intricate. In
real life, and in social interaction, a person may hide infidelity and confess
Islam, while another may have strong faith but have had no access to the
final revelation.

> Of the people there are some who say: We believe in God and the last day;
> but they do not (really) believe. Fain would they deceive God and those
> who believe, but they only deceive themselves, and realize (it) not!
>
> (Baqarah 2:9)

> When you look at them, their exteriors please you; and when they speak, you
> listen to their words. They are as (stiff and hollow) as pieces of timber propped
> up, (unable to stand on their own). They think that every cry is against them.
> They are the enemies; so beware of them. God stands against them. How
> deluded are they (away from the truth)!
>
> (Munafiqun 63:4)

The infidelity that in the Qur'an requires moral indignation and direct
opposition does not simply relate to the misconceptions and misinterpre-
tations resulting from human limitations—it relates to the deliberate
choice to place one's self-inclination and self-gratification over and above
the principles of truth, goodness, and justice.

Therefore, *iman* and *kufr*, or faith and infidelity, cannot, and must not,
be reduced to a question of affiliation and formal association with a particular religion or religious group. They signify two opposing attitudes
and moral commitments, that separate individuals with remarkable compassion and strong commitment to the common good from those given to
selfishness, greed, and callousness. Hence, the Qur'an is specific that
interfaith relations must rest on the principle of mutual recognition and
respect. Ultimately, people must be judged not in terms of what religion
they profess but on the quality of their attitudes and actions.

CHAPTER 10

Calamity and Patience

When calamity afflicts people they often ask why. When the Indian Ocean tsunami disaster caused death and destruction, people asked why—why this much death? When young children get killed or injured because of natural disasters or human tragedy, people ask, why? When good and peaceful people get abused or harmed by criminal gangs or oppressive governments, people ask why. The "why" questions are the most difficult questions a person can ask. Human intelligence does fairly well in answering "how" and "what," but it often does poorly in answering the question of "why," particularly when it comes to the great issues confronting humanity.

Why does God cause people to die? Here is how the Qur'an answers this question: in Surah Mulk, verse two, God says:

> He it is who created death and life that he may try which of you is best in deed, and he is the exalted in might, oft forgiving.
>
> (Mulk 67:2)

Life is a journey in which individuals are tried and tested, and the true character of individuals is revealed for all to see. Nothing reveals the character of a person more than pain, suffering, and calamity, and nothing strengthens and develops the character of a person more profoundly than adversity. It is in maintaining one's composure, principles, values, and commitments that one's moral character evolves and matures.

> Do people think that they will be left alone on saying, we believe, and that they will not be tested? We did test those before them, and God will certainly know those who are true from those who are false.
>
> ('Ankabut 29:2–3)

The test that sets apart those who have deep commitment and strong faith from those whose faith is shallow and shaky takes different shapes and forms. It may take the form of hunger, poverty, loss of dear ones or hard-earned property, or fear for life during periods of turmoil. In Surah Baqarah, verse 55, God reveals:

> Be sure we shall test you with something of fear and hunger, some loss in goods and lives, or the fruits (of your toil), but give glad tidings to those who patiently persevere—those who say, when afflicted with calamity: To God we belong, and to him is our return.
>
> (Baqarah 2:155)

In the struggle to overcome adversity, certain elements are essential: perseverance, deep commitment, and unwavering trust in God and his compassion and mercy.

FROM A DIVINE PERSPECTIVE

The "why" question with regard to calamity was addressed in the story of Musa (Moses) and the wise man, who the Qur'an thus describes: "[He is] one of our servants, on whom we had bestowed mercy from ourselves and whom we had taught knowledge from our own presence" (Kahf 18:65).

Early Muslim exegeses refer to the wise man as Alkhidr, and the Qur'an states that he lived in a place where "two seas meet." Little is known about the identity of Alkhidr, and it is not clear how he became known with this name, given the fact that the Qur'an does not reveal his name. The significance of his story lies in his ability to show Moses that what is seen from the human vantage point as tragic and catastrophic may have deeper meaning if it is looked at from a broader perspective— that is, from a perspective that looks at human events within a larger time frame and social setting.

The story clearly emphasizes that pain and suffering may be a mercy in disguise that forestalls greater evil. What might appear to be tragic and calamitous may hide a greater mercy and good. Moses asked the wise man: "May I follow you, on the ground that you teach me something of the (higher) truth which you have been taught?" (Kahf 18:66). Alkhidr asks Moses to observe him quietly and not to ask questions until he is given clarifications, but then he doubts Moses's ability to remain silent: "You will not be able to have patience with me!" (Kahf 18:67).

Moses promises to be patient and not to ask questions, a promise he soon discovers is too hard to fulfill. Remaining silent is not an option for Moses, particularly in the face of a series of actions that appear excessive, intolerable, and outrageous. The Qur'an narrates three instances in which Moses witnesses bewildering actions by the wise man that include damaging the vessel of poor sailors, killing a child, and repairing a wall without compensation at the outskirts of a village, even after the people of that village refuse to provide them with food they urgently need. Every time the man apparently acts in irrational or inhumane ways, Moses protests loudly, objecting to what he sees as an unacceptable behavior, and every time he promises to stay calm and not ask questions again when the wise man reminds him of his promise. Finally, the wise man decides to end his association with Moses after the latter breaks his promise for the third time. Before departing he reveals to Moses the rationale for his seemingly outrageous behavior:

> As for the boat, it belonged to certain men in dire want: they plied on the water: I but wished to render it unserviceable, for there was after them a certain king who seized on every boat by force. As for the youth, his parents were people of faith, and we feared that he would grieve them by obstinate rebellion and ingratitude. So we intended that their Lord would give them in exchange (a son) better in purity (of conduct) and closer in affection. As for the wall, it belonged to two youths, orphans, in the town; there was, beneath it, a buried treasure, to which they were entitled; their father had been a righteous man: so your Lord desired that they should attain their age of full strength and get out their treasure a mercy (and favor) from your Lord. I did it not of my own accord. Such is the interpretation of (those things) over which you were unable to hold patience.
>
> (Kahf 18:79–82)

Two of Moses's experiences with the wise man give a unique insight into the question of calamity. The damage that was done to the vessel was for sure a calamity from the point of view of the poor sailors, who depended on the vessel to make their living. The damage would require them to put in additional work to repair their vessel and would deprive them from income for days. What the sailors were not aware of was that the calamity they suffered, and the short-term hardship they endured, was essential for preventing far greater calamity and hardship.

Similarly, the death of the child from the point of view of the parents was for sure a calamity and a source of pain and grievance. It was, nonetheless, a calamity that forestalled much greater calamity, that would have brought greater harm to many people, including his parents.

Perhaps the most troubling element in the above story is the death of the child. The child lost his life before reaching the age of maturity and did not experience life in its fullness. The action of the wise man was intolerable to Moses, even though he apparently knew the special gift Alkhidr had and was eager to learn. The Qur'an makes no further reference to the destiny of the boy, other than stressing that both the knowledge and actions of the wise man were divinely inspired.

Moses's experience with Alkhidr is unique and has no other purpose than to help us to gain some insight into the mystery of life. It is intended to help us be more persevering, calm, and hopeful in the face of adversity and calamity, and to have confidence in the wisdom and mercy of God. It shows that, as humans, we must respond to events by being authentic human beings—acting on our personal knowledge and responding to our values and commitments. Like Moses, we cannot but be outraged by the excesses of other human beings, even when they claim "divine inspiration" for their excessive behavior. Even after knowing that Alkhidr was given special insights and knowledge, Moses could only react as an authentic human being.

I do recall hearing an amazing story that has some resemblance with the insight told in the above verses. Hassan Hathout, the well-known writer, philanthropist, and Muslim-American leader shared the story during a meeting in Los Angeles. The story is of a young Egyptian friend of his who had finished his undergraduate studies at the University of Egypt and was admitted to a graduate studies program on scholarship at the reputed Massachusetts Institute of Technology in Boston. On the way to the airport, as he was about to catch his flight to pursue his graduate studies, this young man suffered serious injuries from a car accident and was taken to the hospital. Doctors told him that he would have to spend at least three months in the hospital, and it did not take him long to realize that his exciting plans to pursue his higher education were in ruin. His frustration and disappointment soon dissipated, when he learned few days later that the airplane which he was supposed to take on that "awful" day crashed en route to Boston, and all passengers on board perished. In seconds, his disappointment, restlessness, and sense of loss and abandonment were replaced with calm and a sense of gratitude.

It finally dawned on him that he was very fortunate, despite his loss of a great opportunity, as he reflected on the loss of life of the passengers on the ill-fated flight he missed.

FATE AND DESTINY

The impact of divine action that is intended to influence the direction of social interaction and the evolution of human history brings to the fore the notions of fate (*qada'*) and destiny (*qadar*). Both notions play an important role in the writings of almost all religions, and they are considered to be one of the articles of the Islamic faith. In *hadith* Jibril (Gabriel), which was reported by Bukhari, it says: "'Tell me about faith,' asked the strange man. 'That you should believe in God, his angels, his books, his messengers, and in fate and destiny, both good and evil, is determined by God.'" Both concepts are interrelated and involve the idea of predetermined and preordained events. And both are among the most difficult notions to discuss and elaborate on, but they are essential for deeper understanding of the forces at play in human society and history, as well as for maintaining deep faith and strong trust in divine benevolence, wisdom, and mercy.

Understanding these two nuanced concepts is crucial for maintaining high morale, a strong will, and a forward-looking outlook in the face of mounting challenges and grave adversity. Fate (*qada'*) refers to the divine judgment that predetermines and orders the course of events. Fate defines events as ordered or "meant to be." The divine predetermination is intended to ensure certain outcomes in the evolution of human life, such as the inevitable clash of good and evil, justice and injustice, and right and wrong. Destiny refers, on the other hand, to the impact of divine judgment, or fate, on the life of the individual. Destiny involves consequences of choices and actions, as it relates to particular social settings and the way they affect individual conditions.

The destiny of a person is affected both by the social setting in which a person is born and matures, and his/her personal values and commitments. Unlike fate, though, the notion of destiny places more emphasis on the importance of individual choices in determining the future of the person who makes these choices. As such, fate as a divine judgment does not only direct the life of the individual, but it also responds to it and nurtures it. The concepts of fate and destiny are brought to the fore and aptly illustrated in the story of Prophet Yusuf (Joseph), which is narrated in detail in the Qur'an. Young Joseph grew up in a family of 12 children. He was the 11th child of Prophet Ya'qub (Jacob), but the first child to be born to a second wife when Jacob reached an advanced age. Jacob showed great affection to Joseph and his younger brother Benjamin, and he unwittingly ignited a burning jealousy in the hearts of the older siblings. This situation triggered a series of events that culminated in the appointment of Joseph to the treasury of Egypt and the migration of Jacob's family to Egypt. Prophet Yusuf's story vividly shows how God's design for Israel (Jacob) and his children, as a family destined to establish the monotheistic tradition for millennia to come, was brought to fruition despite the limited vision and aspirations of Jacob's children. Consumed with their personal rivalry, they set out to finish Yusuf once and for all.

Although the initial plan was to kill him, it was instead Yusuf's fate to be thrown into a well and be taken to Egypt as a slave boy, who was sold into the house of the prime minister (Al-Aziz) of Egypt. Throughout his tribulations, Yusuf maintained his moral values and commitments, and he remained true to God. His formative years in the house of Jacob, the son of Isaac and the grandson of Abraham, had given him a profound moral character and unshakable faith in the wisdom, mercy, and power of God. One deep insight into how the divine plan overcomes individual plans and plots is provided in the confrontation between Yusuf and the wife of the prime minister. Faced with the prospect of being lured to the sexual excesses and intrigues of the Egyptian noble class, Yusuf turned to God, asking for guidance and protection from the bad influence he was subjected to. "He said: O my Lord! The prison is more to my liking

than that to which they invite me; unless to turn away their lure, I fear
I will be lured to them and join the rank of the ignorance" (Yusuf 12:33–34).

The response to his prayer came in the form of yet more hardship. He
was sent to prison after the prime minister's wife used her influence in
retaliation for his refusal to succumb to her sexual advances. Paradoxically, it was his imprisonment with the advisor to the king of Egypt,
who, like him, was unjustly thrown in jail, that ultimately gave him access
to the king. Through his advisor, the king became acquainted with Yusuf
and his special skills, leading to Yusuf's appointment as the treasurer of
Egypt, and to the fulfillment of the dream (vision) he shared with his
father when he was a little boy.

PATIENCE AND PERSEVERANCE

Patience is a key theme in the Qur'an and an important quality of the
faithful. Given the fact that pursuing important goals entails overcoming
mounting challenges and difficulties, patience and perseverance is a
crucial ingredient for success.

> O you who believe! Persevere in patience and constancy; vie in such perse-
> verance; strengthen each other; and fear God; that you may succeed.
>
> (Al 'Imran 3:200)

Luqman the wise advised his son to show perseverance and patience,
to pray regularly, and to promote righteousness and justice. Linking these
three important qualities is indeed a reflection of the great knowledge and
wisdom Luqman enjoyed. For if enjoining the right and forbidding corruption is an individual duty, nothing can help the individual more in
maintaining this important social function than seeking spiritual renewal
through prayer, as well as cultivating the ability to stay calm in the face of
retaliation by corrupt people, particularly when those people happen to
enjoy a commanding position in society.

> O my son! Establish regular prayer, enjoin what is just, and forbid what is
> wrong; and bear with patient constancy whatever betide you; for this is
> firmness (of purpose) in (the conduct of) affairs.
>
> (Luqman 31:17)

The importance of both prayer and patience to overcome calamity
and challenges is often stressed in the Qur'an, as the faithful are urged
to resort to both as they pursue their moral obligations and social
responsibilities:

> Nay, seek (God's) help with patient perseverance and prayer: it is indeed
> hard, except to those who are humble with God, who bear in mind the
> certainty that they are to meet their Lord, and that they are to return to him.
>
> (Baqarah 2:45–46)

> O you who believe! Seek help with patient perseverance and prayer: for God
> is with those who patiently persevere.
>
> (Baqarah 2:153)

Patience in the Qur'an does not mean an attitude of "wait and see,"
and it should not be confused, therefore, with inaction. Rather, patience
is a positive attitude and posture that denotes self-discipline and the ability to control one's emotions, so as to avoid frustration and despair when
one's efforts to pursue important goals hit serious obstacles and great
challenges. Patience in the Qur'an equates to constancy, perseverance,
steadfastness, and courage.

> Therefore patiently persevere, as did (all) messengers of resolve; and be in no
> haste about the (unbelievers).
>
> (Ahkaf 46:35)

The "messengers of resolve" were those distinguished with great determination and the ability to persevere in the face of adversity and calamity
in pursuit of their missions. They include prophets like Noah, Abraham,
Joseph, Moses, Jesus, and Muhammad. Not all prophets were able to exert
the same level of patience and perseverance. Prophet Yunus (Jonah), for
instance, was frustrated with his people and their indifference to his call.
He grew more impatient with their apathy and decided to leave his town
and take to the sea. When the ship he was sailing in got rocked by a storm,
he was among those who were selected by lottery to be thrown overboard.
He was eventually saved, when the whale that swallowed him threw him
out near the shore. His ordeal was used in the Qur'an as an example for
the ill consequences of impatience and haste.

> So wait with patience for the command of your Lord, and be not like the
> companion of the fish, when he cried out in agony.
>
> (Qalam 68:48)

The Qur'an thus frequently reminds the faithful of the need to stay
calm in the face of calamity and to persevere in pursuit of good goals
and objectives. Patience is crucial for overcoming adversity and for
success, and the harassment and ill-will of people of corruption and
excess will have no real negative effects on those who patiently persevere
in doing what it is right and just.

> If aught that is good befalls you, it grieves them; but if some misfortune over-
> takes you, they rejoice at it. But if you are constant and do right, not the least
> harm will their cunning do to you; for God encompasses all that they do.
>
> (Al 'Imran 3:120)

Along with deep conviction and strong faith, patience is the hallmark
of true leadership and of leaders who are destined to achieve their goals
and lead their people into success and triumph.

And we appointed, from among them, leaders, giving guidance under our command, so long as they persevered with patience and continued to have faith in our signs.

(Sajdah 32:24)

A SIGN OF PROFOUND FAITH

Given the frustration, pain, and suffering that people endure in life, patience is indeed a great virtue and an essential quality. Patience, properly understood as persistence, constancy, and perseverance, is of particular importance to individuals who want to pursue noble goals and lead others in improving the human condition. Patience is, therefore, presented in the Qur'an as a sign of deep faith. Those who waver and panic in the face of adversity and calamity are deprived of depth of faith. They apparently have not developed the level of trust in God which they need to stay calm in times of turmoil and upheaval. Calamity should only bring noble and sublime emotions (compassion, concern, care, and the like), and never uncontrolled fear, panic, or despair.

If we give man a taste of mercy from ourselves, and then withdraw it from him, behold! He is in despair and (falls into) blasphemy. But if we give him a taste of (our) favors after adversity has touched him, he is sure to say, All evil has departed from me; behold! He falls into exultation and pride. Not so do those who show patience and constancy, and work righteousness; for them is forgiveness (of sins) and a great reward. Perchance you may (feel the inclination) to give up a part of what is revealed to you.

(Hud 11:9–12)

There are among men some who serve God, as it were, on the verge: if good befalls them, they are, therewith, well content; but if a trial comes to them, they turn on their faces; they lose both this world and the hereafter: that is loss for all to see!

(Hajj 22:11)

The above verse was revealed in reference to Shayba bin 'Utbah, who, before converting to Islam, asked the prophet to pray for him to be blessed with wealth and children. The Prophet did. When Shayba accepted Islam, he lost his wealth and was tried in his children, so he renounced his faith. Because patience in the face of calamity is the ultimate sign of strong faith, the Qur'an reserves the greatest reward to people of patience—for they are rewarded beyond accounts and measures:

Those who patiently persevere will truly receive a reward without measure!

(Zumar 39:10)

PART III

INNER PEACE

Inner peace is the outcome of achieving deep faith and the first step in pursuing social and eternal peace. Inner peace is realized through connecting with the Divine and by bringing harmony between the human and divine wills.

The five pillars of Islam are intended for maintaining the human-divine connection, bringing spiritual discipline, and developing devotion to God and the values and notions associated with him. *Taqwa* (consciousness of the Divine) is the key concept stressed throughout the Qur'an for achieving moral integrity and spiritual growth, and the pillars of Islam are the foundation upon which *taqwa* is established and nurtured.

The struggle for achieving inner peace is, therefore, a struggle to submit the human will to the divine will. This struggle is the essence of Islam, whose name signifies the very act of submission to the Divine.

CHAPTER 11

Gratitude and Praise

Praising God is an essential attitude of the people of faith, because it defines the relationship between the Divine and the believer as the servant of God. Praising is, on the one hand, an act of acknowledgment of the good and beneficial qualities possessed by the one who is the object of praise. It is, on the other hand, a reflection of the gratitude felt by the one who receives the intended good. As such, gratitude and praise are complementary qualities that involve the act of goodness and the act of appreciating goodness. Each of the two acts anticipates and invokes the other.

Praising God also defines the relation between God and his creation and is the natural state of every creature, because it is the natural response to the act of creation and the qualities of the creator. The Qur'an tells us that there is nothing, not a thing, but celebrates the praises of God:

> The seven heavens and the earth, and all beings therein, declare his glory: there is not a thing but celebrates his praise; and yet you understand not how they declare his glory! Verily he is oft-forbearing, most forgiving!
> (Isra' 17:44)

Declaring the glory of God is the highest instance of praise that is done by every creature. Human beings may not be aware of the act of praising experienced by other beings, but it is, the Qur'an stresses, an act that is intrinsic to all things.

PRAISING GOD

Praising God (*alhamdulillah*) is a universal sentiment towards the praiseworthy one. The Qur'anic term *"alhamd"* is uniquely directed to God, for only God deserves *alhamd*. For God, and God alone, can both intend goodness and ensure that the goodness is realized. Human beings may intend good to others but end up harming them. And hence it is only

God who is worthy of the ultimate praise, for he is the source of all good, even the good that is effected by other human beings. Praising God makes up the first word in the Qur'an. The word *"alhamd"* is the first word of the opening chapter of the Qur'an:

> Praise to God the cherisher and sustainer of the worlds.
>
> (Fatihah 1:1)

Praising God is the essence of creation. For in creating the universe, God's infinite compassion, knowledge, wisdom, and power were brought to bear on the natural and spiritual orders, that make life in all its details the amazing experience it is, and the source of awe and wonder.

> Praise to God who created heavens and the earth and made the darkness and the light, yet those who reject faith hold (others) as equal with their Guardian Lord.
>
> (An'am 6:1)

Even the thunder celebrates the glory of God, something that the angels do as well—though of course with greater awareness of his majesty, greatness, and infinite power. "Even the thunder celebrates his praises, and so do the angels with awe" (Ra'd 13:13).

Praising God is intrinsic to the very act of divine revelation that was intended to empower humanity with purpose and knowledge. Divine revelation was always an important moment of hope and reform in human history. "Praise to God who revealed the criterion (furqan) to his servant and has allowed therein no crookedness" (Kahf 18:1).

And hence praising God will be the last word on the day of judgment, when all affairs are dispensed with compassion and justice. "The after life experience of the believers would be exceeding satisfying and gratifying that praising God is the conclusion of the prayers of the people of paradise" ('Ankabut 29:75).

> Their last prayer will be: Praises to God the Master of the Worlds.
>
> (Yunus 10:10)

SHOWING GRATITUDE

God deserves praise because he is praiseworthy, because his qualities are praiseworthy, and because his actions are praiseworthy. The praises he deserves emanate for his divine qualities that make his act of creation and revelation worthy of praise. But praising God is only the beginning, as the believer who declares his or her faith in God and asserts his or her commitment to a covenant with the Divine must also show gratitude. Showing gratitude is what the Qur'an describes as the act of *shukr*. As such, *alhamd* (praising God) and *shukr* (showing gratitude), though inter-related, are two distinct acts. To praise is to acknowledge God's qualities, to show gratitude, on the other hand, is to positively respond to the divine act of goodness.

> He strengthened you with his aid and gave you things for sustenance, that you might be grateful.
>
> (Anfal 8:26)

> And gave you hearing, sight, and intelligence that you might be grateful.
>
> (Sajdah 32:9)

Human beings are expected to show gratitude in response to the many favors bestowed on them by the compassionate and merciful God. *Shukr* as an act of gratitude is thus the opposite of *kufr*, which is an act of ingratitude.

> Then do you remember me; I will remember you. Be grateful to me and reject not faith.
>
> (Baqarah 2:152)

THE PRIVILEGE OF GRATITUDE

God is praiseworthy, and his praiseworthiness is in need of no human acknowledgement. Among God's intelligent creatures, it is indeed the angels that are in a constant and continuous state of gratitude and appreciation of God's glory:

> To him belong all (creatures) in the heavens and on earth: even those who are in his (very) presence are not too proud to serve him, nor are they (ever) weary (of his service): they celebrate his praises night and day, nor do they ever flag or intermit.
>
> (Anbiya' 21:19–20)

Human beings have, by and large, failed to value and appreciate God's majesty and glory the way he should be valued and appreciated:

> No just estimate have they made of God, such as is due to him: on the day of judgment the whole of the earth will be but his handful, and the heavens will be rolled up in his right hand: glory to him! High is he above the partners they attribute to him!
>
> (Zumar 39:67)

Praising God and expressing gratitude for the many favors he has bestowed on humanity is, therefore, a human privilege. The benefits drawn from this intellectual, emotional, and spiritual exercise belong to the human being. For the feeling of gratitude frees the human being from the negative energy generated when people fail to see the many favors God has bestowed on them. Even the most unprivileged human being would be able to count numerous favors God has bestowed on him. The positive energy generated, on the other hand, from a healthy sense of gratitude, can sustain the human being in the face of the greatest adversity and can inspire one to hope for more favors.

> We bestowed wisdom on Luqman: show your gratitude to God; any who is so grateful does so to the benefit of his own soul, but if any is ungrateful, verily God is free of all wants, worthy of all praises.
>
> (Luqman 31:12)

A healthy sense of gratitude inspires people to work hard to express their gratitude and hence help themselves, increasing their chances to lead a successful life away from frustrations and the negative feeling of being abandoned. As people express their gratitude and act out of a grateful attitude, they stand to receive greater gifts, opportunities, and improvements.

> And remember! Your Lord caused be declared: If you are grateful, I will increase my favors to you, and if you show ingratitude, truly my punishment is terrible indeed.
>
> (Ibrahim 41:7)

There are countless examples in the Qur'an of the positive fruits of a grateful attitude, from the life of prophets and godly individuals. The life and struggle of Prophet Yusuf, which the Qur'an relates in great detail, is perhaps the most telling and inspiring.

INTRINSIC GOOD IN APPARENT EVIL

God is praiseworthy even when his acts cause harm! This is because harm is not intended for itself or for personal gain, but rather it is often a transient pain that is followed by greater opportunities and great rewards. The Qur'an depicts human experience as a set of trials whose pain and suffering are intrinsic to a life of faith and growth.

> O you humans! Verily you are ever toiling on towards your Lord—painfully toiling—but you shall meet him.
>
> (Inshiqaq 84:6)

Toil is the lot of all people, but those who stick to their values and beliefs are bound to experience more trying times:

> Do men think that they will be left alone on saying, we believe, and that they will not be tested? We did test those before them, and God will certainly know those who are true from those who are false.
>
> ('Ankabut 29:2–3)

Pain and pleasure, sadness and happiness, or difficulty and ease, are never given in pure form to any particular human being but always come together in either rapid or occasional succession.

> Verily, with every difficulty, there is relief.
>
> (Inshirah 94:5)

One of the most inspiring examples of struggle and perseverance that, combined with gratitude, brought great rewards, is that of Prophet Yusuf. I referred elsewhere (see Calamity and Patience) to the series of trials through which Yusuf matured into the exemplary man he was. I do not want to repeat the detailed analysis of Yusuf's struggle but would rather focus on one incident in his struggle that illustrates how his gratitude, even in the face of the most trying times, was essential for his rise and success.

When Yusuf turned to God, seeking his support and protection from the temptations he was subjected to by the women of the upper Egyptian social class, his prayers were accepted. Yusuf was spared the temptations, however, by being thrown into jail. Rather than complaining about the high cost he had to pay for escaping the sinful lure, he accepted with gratitude his fate:

> He said: O my Lord! The prison is more to my liking than that to which they invite me; unless to turn away their lure, I fear I will be lured to them and join the rank of the ignorance.
>
> (Yusuf 12:33–34)

Yet the prison sentence was part of greater plan he was hardly aware of, for it was during his prison time that he became acquainted with a high-ranking Egyptian official who was put in jail as part of palace intrigues. The Egyptian official became aware of Yusuf's special gifts, and he recommended him to the king of Egypt, who, upon experiencing Yusuf's profound knowledge and insights, appointed him as his treasurer. Prophet Muhammad expressed the fruits of gratitude in an insightful way:

> How wonderful is the condition of the person who submits to God's will (the Muslim), for his condition is always good: when happiness comes his way he is grateful, and this is good for him; and when calamity befalls him he is patient, and that is good for him.
>
> (Reported by Imam Muslim)

CHAPTER 12

Reconnecting through Prayer

P rayer is the second most important pillar of Islam, second in importance only to the declaration of faith. Prayer for Muslims take two interrelated forms: the prescribed prayer (*salah*) and supplication (*du'a*). Both *salah* and *du'a* provide the Muslim with an occasion to directly communicate with God. The two modes of communication complement one another, since *du'a* provides a free form of communication, while *salah* provides a more structured and engaging mode of communication with the Divine.

Salah belongs to a group of symbolic acts known as rituals or *sha'air*. *Sha'air*, literally meaning "marks" or "symbols," are acts of faith. They represent procedures, a series of acts performed for the pleasure of God. These are symbolic acts that invoke in those who perform them a sense of the Divine, help worshipers draw closer to their spiritual source, and increase their commitments to embrace the divine will and divine teachings, even when they fail to understand their full meaning and implications.

Rituals have symbolic meanings because the meaning they provide is not simply intellectual but is, for the most, part spiritual and emotional. When performed properly and sincerely, the ritual of *salah* provides those who practice it regularly with inner fulfillment and experience that can be fully comprehended only by the person performing the *salah*. It is reported that the Prophet considered *salah* as an occasion for relaxation and relief from daily pressures, and he used to ask Bilal to call for prayer by saying, "Relieve us with the prayer O Bilal!"

AN INTENSE SPIRITUAL MOMENT

Prayer is an intense spiritual moment reconnecting humans with the Divine. This reconnection happens in the process of affirming one's faith in, and commitment to, God, and it prepares the believers to receive direction and admonition from their Lord. The formal prayer, or *salah*, consists of certain bodily movements, such as bowing and prostrating, which symbolize a state of submission to God. It also involves recitation of verses of the Qur'an, and hence recalling divine teachings and admonitions.

The essence of the divine-human communication that takes place during prayer is epitomized in the opening surah (Fatihah) of the Qur'an, which is read at least 17 times during the 5 mandatory daily prayers.

> In the name of God, most compassionate, most merciful.
> Praise be to God, the Cherisher and Sustainer of the worlds;
> Most compassionate, most merciful;
> Master of the day of judgment.
> You do we worship, and your aid we seek,
> Show us the straight way,
> The way of those on whom you have bestowed your grace,
> Those whose (portion) is not wrath,
> And who go not astray.
>
> (Fatihah 1:1–7)

In the first half of the surah, believers affirm their faith in God and express gratitude toward him, while in the second half, they ask for guidance and help.

In order to maintain focus on the meaning expressed during the prayer, Muslims are required to come to prayer in a clean body and clear mind. Even before the consumption of alcohol was prohibited, Muslims were instructed to stay away from alcohol around prayer times so they could be conscious of their communication with the Divine and would be able to reconnect to their source.

> O you who believe! Approach not prayers with a mind befogged until you can understand all that you say; nor in a state of ceremonial impurity (except when passing by), until after washing your whole body.
>
> (Nisa' 4:43)

The fact that prayers must be performed at allotted times spread throughout the day ensures that the believers are constantly connected with the Divine and conscious of their moral responsibilities towards him. The Qur'an stresses the importance of performing prayers on time, and in a state of concentration and sobriety:

> Guard strictly your (habit of) prayers, especially the middle prayer; and stand before God in a devout (frame of mind).
>
> (Baqarah 2:238)

The Qur'an also considers failure to maintain regularity and focus as a sign of weak faith and weak commitment to moral values. Lack of interest in prayers may also be a sign of hypocrisy and duplicity:

> The hypocrites think they are over reaching God but he will over-reach them: when they stand up to prayer, they stand without earnestness, to be seen by people, but little do they hold God in remembrance.
>
> (Nisa' 4:142)

It is, indeed, evident that the Qur'an does not see prayer as an isolated act of worship, disconnected from attitudes and moral behavior in the day-to-day concerns of the Muslim, but rather it is an intrinsic part of character building.

PRAYER ESSENTIAL FOR STRENGTHENING FAITH

Prayer is a precondition for both comprehending the divine message and succeeding in the struggle to overcome falsehood and wrongdoing.

> This is the book in which is guidance to the God-conscious; who believe in the unseen, are steadfast in prayer, and spend out of what we have provided for them.
>
> (Baqarah 2:3)

Prayer, the Qur'an stresses, is essential for receiving guidance, as it ensures that the believer is constantly conscious of the divine presence. Such a state of consciousness is crucial to avoiding temptation that leads human beings to error:

> Prayer restrains from shameful and unjust deeds.
>
> ('Ankabut 29:45)

> But after them there followed a posterity who missed prayers and followed after lusts soon, then, will they face destruction.
>
> (Maryam 19:59)

Evidently, prayer is not seen from the Qur'anic perspective as an end in itself, but as a means to maintain the integrity of human beings by reconnecting them to their spiritual source. Therefore, when humans neglect reestablishing this connection through prayer, they end up losing their souls:

> Have you seen the one who denies the judgment (to come)? Then such as the person who repulses the orphan (with harshness), and encourages not the feeding of the indigent. So woe to the worshippers who are neglectful of their prayers; those who (want but) to be seen by people, but refuse (to supply) (even) neighborly needs.
>
> (Ma'un 107:1–7)

And as prayer helps the believers resist temptation, it also strengthens their resolve and gives them the inner peace to stay calm in difficult and challenging times:

> O you who believe! Seek help with patient perseverance and prayer; for God is with those who patiently persevere.
>
> (Baqarah 2:153)

PRAYER KEY FOR MAINTAINING JUSTICE

In addition to strengthening faith, regular prayers help ensure that people are always mindful of their responsibilities before God and reduce the possibility that they will be completely immersed in their pursuit of self-interest without regard to the principles of right and justice:

> Say: My Lord has commanded justice; and that you set your whole selves (to him) at every time and place of prayer, and call upon him, making your devotion sincere as in his sight: such as he created you in the beginning, so shall you return.
>
> (A'raf 7:29)

> O my son! Establish regular prayer, enjoin what is just, and forbid what is wrong: and bear with patient constancy whatever betide you; for this is firmness (of purpose) in (the conduct of) affairs.
>
> (Luqman 31:17)

> Those [the believers] who hearken to their Lord, and establish regular prayer; who (conduct) their affairs by mutual consultation; who spend out of what we bestow on them for sustenance.
>
> (Shura 42:38)

In the above *ayahs*, prayer is directly linked to the maintenance of justice, the promotion of right, and maintaining egalitarian social and political order through *shurah,* or mutual consultation.

PRAYER CENTRAL TO LEADERSHIP

Given the importance of prayer in reconnecting the human being with God and the values associated with him, and given the fact that prayer is central to the character formation of the faithful, leaders who take upon themselves the difficult task of confronting corruption and promoting good and justice are in dire need of the moral and spiritual fortitude that comes with prayer. The Qur'an stresses that those who are entrusted with the epoch-making act of reforming social conditions at crucial junctures of history are people who are given to compassion, justice, and spirituality; qualities that come through deliberate communication with, and by connecting to the source of, compassion, justice, and spiritual life.

> And we made them leaders, guiding (people) by our command, and we sent them inspiration to do good deeds, to establish regular prayers, and to practice regular charity; and they constantly served us (and us only).
>
> (Anbiya' 21:73)

> (They are) those who, if we establish them in the land, establish regular prayer and give regular charity, enjoin the right and forbid wrong: with God rests the end (and decision) of (all) affairs.
>
> (Hajj 22:41)

PRAYER IN CONGREGATION

In a community that is informed by the Qur'an, prayer is not simply an isolated act of worship, but rather it is an institution that defines the character of the Muslim community. The mosque is the center of community life, and the experience of the American Muslim community testifies to that. Throughout North America, mosques are called "Islamic centers."

Prayer is not something that can be confined to individual performance, but it is a collective experience that brings community members together. The Qur'an talks about the "establishment" of prayer, not just the act of prayer. And the Prophet stressed the importance of congregational prayers and made that practice the centerpiece of community life.

> The mosques of God shall be visited and maintained by such as believe in God and the last day, establish regular prayers, and practice regular charity, and fear none (at all) except God. It is they who are expected to be on true guidance.
>
> (Tawbah 9:18)

CHAPTER 13

Moral Discipline and Fasting

Fasting, particularly during the month of Ramadan, is an important experience for nurturing moral commitment and discipline. Muslims refrain from eating, drinking, and sexual intercourse from dawn to dusk for the duration of Ramadan. For some, fasting may appear as a form of deprivation and of bodily exertion. On one level, abstaining from sensual needs and pleasures is indeed a physical experience. But those who stop at the physical aspects of fasting miss the essence of Ramadan and its purpose.

MORAL EXCELLENCE

Ramadan fasting, like other religious practices in Islam, is an occasion for pursuing moral excellence that can also be translated into excellence in social organization and interaction.

The essence of fasting, the month of Ramadan, and its goal is summed in the Qur'an in one word: *taqwa*. "O you who believe! Fasting is prescribed to you as it was prescribed to those before you, that you may attain *taqwa*" (Baqarah 2:183).

But what is *taqwa*? And how does it relate to the physical act of fasting?

Taqwa is a Qur'anic term denoting the state of mind of the faithful who fears God and makes a conscious effort to be mindful of his glory and presence. *Taqwa* is a recurring theme of paramount value that the Qur'an emphasizes time and time again; *taqwa* is both an attitude and a process. It is the attitude that reveals one's commitment to the basic Qur'anic values of courage, generosity, compassion, honesty, steadfastness, and cooperation in pursuing what is right and true. And it is the process by which Muslims internalize these very values and develop their Islamic character.

Thus the Qur'an reminds the believers that they should not reduce religious practices to a set of rituals, of religiously ordained procedures performed at the level of material consciousness. It also reminds them to always be mindful that religious practices like praying and fasting ultimately aim at bringing about moral and spiritual uplifting. As the following Qur'anic verse makes clear:

> It is not righteousness that you turn your faces towards east or west: but it is righteousness to believe in God and the last day, and the angels, the book, and the messengers; to give out of the things you hold dear to your kin, the orphans, the needy, the wayfarer, the one who asks, and to free the slave. And to be steadfast in prayer and to give for charity. To fulfil the contracts you have made, and to be firm and patient in times of pain, adversity, and panic. Such are the people of truth, and such are the *mutaqin*.
>
> (Qur'an 2:177)

As Ramadan helps us to develop our moral discipline, it also reminds us of the plight of those who live in constant hunger and deprivation. We are reminded, time and again, by the revealed book that religiosity is meaningless and pointless if it does not lead people to care and share. "Have you seen one who belies judgment; it is the one who repulses the orphan, and does not insist on feeding the needy. So woe to those who pray but are neglectful of their prayers. Those who are guilty of duplicity and refuse to provide for the ones in need" (Qur'an 107:1–7).

In a tradition that was reported in the books of Bukhari and Muslim on the authority of Abu Hurayra, the Prophet was once asked: "O messenger of God! Who is the most honored of people? He said: The one who has most *taqwa*. They said: This is not what we are asking about. ...He said: ...The best of them prior to Islam is the best of them in Islam if they comprehend (the message of Islam)."

It is not difficult to see that the Prophet's companions did not have immediate access to the meaning of *taqwa*, as many Muslims today still do not. When they did not accept his first statement as an answer, he gave them an explanation of what he meant when he responded to their inquiry about "the most honored of people." In responding with the notion of *taqwa* to the question about "the most honored," the Prophet was reiterating the very meaning provided by the Qur'an: "Verily the most honored of you in the sight of God is the most righteous (*mutaqi*)" (Hujurat 49:13). The Prophet's statement underscores the fact that *taqwa* as a moral and spiritual quality is significant insofar as it leads people to act with benevolence to others.

A CONDITION FOR GUIDANCE

Ramadan fasting helps us attain *taqwa*, the discipline and attitude essential for making sound judgment. As fasting strengthens our spiritual commitments, it liberates us from our narrow interests and self-importance, making us more open to and capable of abiding by universal principles, hence more open to and capable of comprehending divine revelation. Therefore, the Qur'an points out that receiving the revealed word presupposes an attitude of *tawqa*, presupposes *mutaqin*, that is, persons who have the character of *taqwa*:

> This is the book, in it is guidance sure, without doubt, to those who are *mutaqin*.
>
> (Baqarah 2:2)

> But verily this is a message/reminder for the *mutaqin*.
>
> (Haqqah 69:48)

Indeed, Muslims throughout the world, following the example of the Prophet, combine fasting with public prayers in which the Qur'an is recited throughout the month of Ramadan. The Prophet used to dedicate the month of Ramadan, the month in which the Qur'an was first revealed, to undertake a complete review the book. Today Muslims the world over strive to do the same by devoting their night prayers to make a complete reading of the Qur'an.

A SOURCE OF STRENGTH AND EMPOWERMENT

Nothing does empower a community more than the development of the moral character of its people. By embodying the moral values of revelation, people can have a higher social life, one that is based on mutual respect and help, as it is based on honest and fair dealings, as well as a sense of duty that encourages people to observe the principles of right and justice as they pursue their varying and competing interests. The theme that a moral life based on the notion of *taqwa* leads to societal strength and prosperity is oft repeated in the Qur'an:

> Whoever has *taqwa* of God, he prepares a way out for them, and he provides them from sources they never could imagine.
>
> (Talaq 65:2–3)

> Verily the earth is God's to give as a heritage to such of his servants as he pleases; and the end is best for the *mutaqin*.
>
> (A'raf 7:128)

PHYSICAL AND MORAL DISCIPLINE

Fasting is not simply a time during which people deprive themselves from physical pleasures but is an occasion to exercise moral restraint as well. The Prophet reportedly said:

> A fasting person should not swear or quarrel, and if any one swore at him or quarreled with him should say: I am fasting.
>
> (Agreed upon)

Whoever does not quit lying or false witnessing, God does not need him to quit his food and drink.

(Reported by Bukhari)

CLOSER TO GOD

Let me conclude by reminding everyone that Ramadan is a time of remembrance of God and renewal of commitment to the high and noble values he prescribed to mankind—and nothing would give us a sense of spiritual fulfillment more than the state of *taqwa* that Ramadan helps us to realize.

> Behold! Verily on the friends of God there is no fear, nor shall they grieve: those who believe and exercise *taqwa*.

(Yunus 10:62–63)

The Prophet told that God said: "All the good deeds of the children of Adam will be rewarded in multiplicity: ten to seven hundred times, except fasting: it is for me and I will give unspecified reward for it: A person leaves his pleasures and food for me. The fasting person has two moments of pleasure: one when he breaks his fast, and one when he meets his Lord" (Muslim).

Fasting is not simply a time during which people deprive themselves from physical pleasures, but it is also an occasion to exercise moral restraint and experience spiritual growth. Ramadan is a time of remembrance of God and renewal of commitment to the high and noble values he revealed to mankind. And nothing would give us a sense of spiritual fulfillment more than the state of *taqwq*, of God-consciousness, that fasting helps us to realize.

CHAPTER 14

Purification through Giving

Giving is sweeter, nobler, and more rewarding than taking. This is a divine principle that permeates revelation and existence, one succinctly expressed by Prophet Muhammad: "the upper hand is better than the lower hand."

Giving is a means for both spiritual growth and social justice. It helps the individual overcome the negative energy that results from personal attachment to property and wealth, as it helps society to attend to the needs of the least fortunate. As such, it sets society and social life on a foundation of compassion, mutual help, and mutual respect.

The most regular and demanded form of giving is known as *zakah*, a Qur'anic term that literally means "purity." *Zakah* is required of every believing man and woman whose income is beyond his or her essential needs.

> The believers, men and women, are protectors, one of another: they enjoin what is just, and forbid what is evil: they observe regular prayers, practice regular charity (*zakah*), and obey God and his messenger. On them will God pour his mercy: for God is exalted in power, wise.
>
> (Tawbah 9:71)

Zakah, as a regular charity to be taken out of the surplus income of all individuals and businesses, is due to people of limited means. The Qur'an specifies six categories of individuals who are entitled to the *zakah* money:

> Alms are for the poor and the needy, and those employed to administer the (funds); for those whose hearts have been (recently) reconciled (to the truth); for those in bondage and in debt; in the way of God; and for the wayfarer: (thus is it) ordained by God, and God is full of knowledge and wisdom.
>
> (Tawbah 9:60)

Zakah must be spent for catering to the needs of the six categories specified in the above verse. These include the poor, who are deprived of all income either because their health and physical conditions do not allow them to work, or because they have no jobs and regular income. The needy are individuals whose income is insufficient to fulfill their essential needs. Those who work full time or part time in charity organizations that collect *zakah* funds and distribute the collected funds can also be paid from the *zakah* money so long as that is done in a fair and equitable way.

Zakah can also be paid to individuals who have just joined the faith community and need support as they struggle to reconcile themselves with their new conditions and situations. A person who is overwhelmed with debt has claim to the *zakah* money, as does a traveler who has lost or run out of the money he or she needs to get back home. The final category is left open to any good action or deed that reaffirms Islamic values and principles, for this money is to be spent in the "way of God."

SPIRITUAL GROWTH

Spiritual growth lies in ensuring that one is able to act on the qualities intrinsic to the human spirit, such as justice, compassion, faithfulness, love, generosity, care, and the like. Similar to human physical capacities, spiritual capacities need to be exercised to grow. Muscular, mental, and spiritual capacities do not grow unless they are constantly exercised, and when they are not used for a while they will surely deteriorate.

Every human being is born with the capacity, and hence the potential, to become a compassionate, caring, generous, loving, and giving person. It is the person's choice to exercise these capacities and use intrinsic human qualities in ways that lead to their realization through nourishment, or to their deterioration through neglect. Human spirit is, further, susceptible to temptation and corruption as it is lured and afflicted by its social surrounding, which is never in a state of perfection. One important way of purifying the human spirit after it is corrupted by earthly lures is through acts of charity. Giving out of the provisions that one has is an act of purification of the self and cleansing of the human spirit from the seeds of sin.

> Of their goods take alms, that so you might purify and sanctify them; and pray on their behalf, verily your prayers are a source of security for them: and God is one who hears and knows.
>
> (Tawbah 9:103)

Giving for the pleasure of God does not only strengthen one's faith; it also ensures that one is not attached to property and wealth but is instead able to give out of the provisions he or she has, in order to make a difference in the lives of others. For this reason, the Qur'an encourages the faithful to give out of the things that are dear to them:

O you who believe! Give out of the good things which you have (honorably) earned, and of the fruits of the earth which we have produced for you, and do not even aim at getting anything which is bad, in order that out of it you may give away something, when you yourselves would not receive it except with closed eyes. And know that God is free of all wants, and worthy of all praise.

(Baqarah 2:267)

By no means shall you attain righteousness unless you give (freely) of that which you love; and whatever you give, of a truth God knows it well.

(Al 'Imran 3:92)

Charitable spending, the Qur'an stresses, does not lead to any decrease of wealth. On the contrary, it results in the blessing of one's provisions and wealth. What decreases wealth is, paradoxically, greed and the desire to resort to usurious and exploitative means to increase one's wealth.

SOCIAL JUSTICE

Social justice is about both providing hope and opportunities to those who urgently need them, as well as displaying concern for, and interest in, social solidarity and common good. An important measure of social vitality, and the potential for development and growth, is the extent to which those who are gifted with provisions and means are willing to shoulder the least fortunate and help them to overcome their conditions of adversity. On the other hand, the exploitation of the poor by the rich is a sign of social decline and the breaking up of the social fabric that holds society together.

God devastates usury but gives increase for charity; for he loves not the ungrateful and wicked.

(Baqarah 2:267)

The Prophet reconfirmed this meaning when he told his companion: "No wealth decreases because of charity spending." The Qur'an uses the metaphor of the wheat or corn grain to underscore the same point; when the wheat grain is given back to the soil rather than being consumed by the person who possesses it, it multiplies exponentially:

The parable of those who spend their substance in the way of God is that of a grain of corn: it grows seven ears, and each ear has a hundred grains. God gives manifold increase to whom he pleases: and God cares for all and he knows all things.

(Baqarah 2:261)

The multiple rewards are both of this life and the hereafter. Spending can multiply income and wealth in this life and will multiply rewards in the hereafter. It is a social and historical fact that societies that have lesser economic disparity between the "haves" and "have-nots" often do much better socially and economically than those in which the disparity is great.

The Qur'an repeatedly reminds people of the interconnectedness between the social and spiritual. It is not sufficient alone to give out of one's personal wealth to bring about more just and equitable society, but rather charity must be based on an attitude of compassion, even humility.

> Those who spend their substance in the way of God, and follow not up their gifts with reminders of their generosity or with injury, for them their reward is with their Lord; on them shall be no fear, nor shall they grieve. Kind words and the covering of faults are better than charity followed by injury. God is free of all wants, and he is most forbearing.
>
> (Baqarah 2:262–263)

A kind word is better than an act of charity followed by hurting and humiliating words, for charity is at heart a matter of attitude. The right attitude that leads to the true act of charity is one that recognizes that the human possession of property is a temporary and transient matter, and that, ultimately, the earth and all its provisions belong to God. It is God who gave people the power and opportunity to take temporary possession, and it is only fitting that those who are endowed see themselves as human agents of the Divine, sharing with those in need with gratitude and humility.

> Believe in God and his messenger, and spend (in charity) out of the (substance) whereof he has made you heirs. For those of you who believe and spend (in charity) is a great reward.
>
> (Hadid 57:7)

GIVING BEYOND NEEDS

Zakah is the minimal financial giving required by the Qur'an, but it is not the only type of giving available to people. In its highest form, giving may include giving any income beyond personal and familial needs. The Prophet and his companions, of whom a significant number were well to do, practiced this type of giving. It is reported that when the Prophet asked his companions to help support the Muslim army that was prepared to repulse the Byzantine army in Northern Arabia, the companions showed an unwavering commitment for giving. Tirmidhi reported their response: "Umar brought half of his wealth, and the Prophet asked him: What have you left to your family? He said: As much as I brought. Then Abu Bakr brought every thing he possessed, and when the Prophet asked: What have you left to your family, Abu Bakr responded: I left for them God and his messenger" (Tirmidhi and Abu Dawud). The Qur'an's, and by implication, the Prophet's, attitude toward wealth is not one of repudiation but one of appreciation and encouragement. The best example of a person who shuns the glares and lures of life is not one who chooses poverty and a life with limited means. Rather, it is a person who works hard to increase personal and collective wealth, but who is constantly able to purify his spirit and intention though acts of giving, spending, and charity.

The Qur'anic emphasis on giving, and the Prophet's encouragement for Muslims to give, was so great that some of the less fortunate companions of the Prophet complained about their inability to match in good deeds those endowed with wealth. They expressed their concern that they would not be able to get the great rewards restored to the good givers:

> Abu Dhar said that a group of the Prophet's companions told the Prophet, God's peace and blessing with him: The people of great wealth get the greatest rewards: they pray as we do, and fast as we do, but are able to spend out of the surplus of their income. He said: Did not God give you things to give in charity: there is charity in every word of glorification of God, humility towards him, gratitude to him, or affirmation of his oneness; in enjoining the right and confronting evil; even there is charity in your sexual intercourse with your wives. They asked: Would we get reward for attaining our pleasure? He said: Do you see if one does that unlawfully, would not he incur sin; so if he does it lawfully he receives reward.
>
> (Reported by Muslim)

In another *hadith* that was reported by Abu Dawud on the authority of Ibad bin Ibad, the Prophet mentions picking away garbage and debris from the road as an instance of charity.

While social justice, and helping those who need and require help, is the goal of charity, the Qur'an always emphasizes the common-sense principle that "charity starts at home."

> ...to spend of your substance, out of love for him, for your kin, for orphans, for the needy, for the wayfarer, for those who ask, and for the ransom of slaves.
>
> (Baqarah 2:177)

It is worth noting that the Qur'an leaves room for charity to anyone who asks, regardless of their social and financial background. The Qur'an directs the believers to give to "those who ask." It is possible that a person with good social and economic background could feel the need for help, so as to be able to overcome a moment of difficulty. One should not dismiss right off the request for help on the assumption that the person who asks is apparently in no need. It is in compliance with the Qur'an that one should consider any request for help by further examining the basis of the expressed need. Giving is essential for addressing the needs of those who require help. It is an important tool for promoting social justice and nourishing a compassionate society. But above all, giving is indispensable for true and profound spiritual growth.

CHAPTER 15

Life's Ultimate Spiritual Journey

*H*ajj, the pilgrimage to Makkah, is one of life's greatest spiritual journeys. It is a journey through time and space, as it is a journey through faith. The rituals of *hajj* reaffirm basic divine values and beliefs, as they reaffirm the founding acts of Ibrahim (Abraham) and his wife Hajar (Haggar) that gave rise to the community of faith in the Islamic tradition.

Hajj is an intense spiritual moment that has its roots in the profound devotion Ibrahim displayed as he was searching for true faith. It is rooted in the long journey Ibrahim took with his wife Hajar and his first child Isma'il (Ishmael) from the Holy Land to the valley of Makkah, the home of the Sacred House, the first house ever devoted to the worship of the One God.

THE SACRED HOUSE

Ibrahim was directed to found the Sacred House in Makkah, a hilly site deprived of any vegetation or water source. The Qur'an narrates Ibrahim's description of the Makkan valley where he left his wife and his infant son:

> O our Lord! I have made some of my offspring to dwell in a valley without cultivation, by the Sacred House; in order, O our Lord, that they may establish regular prayer: so fill the hearts of some with love towards them, and feed them with fruits: so that they may show gratitude.
>
> (Ibrahim 41:37)

In commenting on the above verse, Altabari, the great Muslim historian and exegesist, reports on the authority of Ibn Abbas that Ibrahim made the above *du'a* (prayer) at the valley of Kida' near Makkah, as he was preparing to leave behind the two beloved souls he brought to this lifeless place and to return to the Holy Land. Altabari also reports the following exchange between Ibrahim and Hajar, as he was about to leave:

> To what do you leave us? To what food do you leave us? To what drink do you leave us? Hajar repeatedly asked. When Ibrahim remained silent in the face of her agonizing questions, she then asked him the ultimate question: Did God command you to do this? He replied: Yes. She said: He then would never forsake us.

Ibrahim's painful journey led to the establishment of the city of Makkah out in the middle of nowhere, in the middle of the Arabian desert. Hajar's painful search for people and provisions led, likewise, to the commencement of one of the essential rituals of *hajj:* the walking back and forth between the hills of Safa and Marwa by every pilgrim. Every Muslim who performs *hajj* is required to follow the footsteps of Hajar between the Safa and Marwa hills, walking and jogging back and forth seven times.

God did not, indeed, forsake Hajar and her son Isma'il, and soon water gushed in the middle of the Makkan valley, near the spot where she left her infant as she was jogging from one hill to another in search for provisions and helping hands, thereby ensuring that the helpless mother and her child would have the chance to live. And God did respond to Ibrahim's prayers, as the tribe of Jorhum was attracted by the amazing scene of the blossoming life of an infant with his young mother, sitting next to a gushing spring in the middle a lifeless valley. Little did they know that this lifeless and lonely place would soon become full of life, indeed the liveliest place in the whole of Arabia, if not the entire planet, attracting multitudes of peoples from every imaginable place.

Ibrahim retuned many years later to Makkah to see his wife and grown-up son and to build, with the help of the young Isma'il, the foundation of the Sacred House or *Ka'bah* (the cube-shaped building) at the center of Makkah.

> And remember when Ibrahim and Isma'il raised the foundations of the House (with this prayer): Our Lord! Accept (this service) from us: for you are the all-hearing, the all-knowing. Our Lord! Make of us Muslims bowing to your (will); and of our progeny a people Muslim, bowing to your (will); and show us our places for the celebration of (due) rites; and turn unto us (in mercy); for you are the Oft-Returning, Most Merciful. Our Lord! Send amongst them a messenger of their own, who shall rehearse your signs to them and instruct them in scripture and wisdom, and sanctify them: for you are the Exalted in Might, the Wise.
>
> (Baqarah 2:127–129)

The Sacred House remains today, over three millennia since it was founded, the focal place to which an increasing number of people return every year.

Behold! We gave the site, to Ibrahim, of the (Sacred) House, (saying): Associate not anything (in worship) with me; and sanctify my House for those who compass it round, or stand up, or bow, or prostrate themselves (therein in prayer); and proclaim the pilgrimage (*hajj*) among people; they will come to you on foot and (mounted) on every kind of camel, lean on account of journeys through deep and distant mountain highways; that they may witness the benefits (provided) for them, and celebrate the name of God, through the days appointed, over the cattle which he has provided for them (for sacrifice): then eat you thereof and feed the distressed ones in want. Then let them complete the rites prescribed for them, perform their vows, and (again) circumambulate the ancient House.

(Hajj 22:26–30)

The foundations of the Sacred House are now set in place, and the time has come for people to leave their houses and dwellings and hasten to the house of God, to remember his beautiful names and his favors, and to reaffirm their commitments to him. The call for *hajj* is a call to all Muslims to embark on the journey of a lifetime, to retreat away from their earthly concerns, and to completely devote themselves to God for days. The *hajj*, with its symbolic acts and shared rituals, is an experience of a lifetime. Muslims are required to perform the *hajj*, if they are physically and financially capable of doing so, once in a lifetime. Yet many cherish the privilege of repeating the experience, as they often return to the Sacred House to relive the unique spiritual moment.

Most Muslims go to *hajj* unaware of the extraordinary experience they are about to live, as they rehearse the various rites, chants, and procedures. Reading, learning, and memorizing those rites and chants are one thing, but experiencing them firsthand with countless people is a completely different matter. The *hajj* rites are so rich in symbolic meanings that living them during the days of *hajj* brings intense moments of emotion and spiritual awakening and renewal.

THE RITUALS OF *HAJJ*

The *hajj* rituals were set long before Prophet Muhammad was commissioned to deliver the final revelation to humanity. The rituals were practiced by Ibrahim and Isma'il and those who followed them, also known as *Alahnaf*. Few of Ibrahim's followers could still be found when Prophet Muhammad received his first revelation. The verses of Surah 2 (Baqarah) and Surah 14 (Hajj) outline the rites of *hajj*. The Qur'an specifies the basic rituals of *hajj*, which include (1) *ihram*, or putting on the *hajj* outfit with the intention to begin the ritual, (2) *tawaf*, or circumambulating the Sacred House, (3) *sa'i*, or the walk between two designated hills, (4) *wuquf* (standing) on Mount Arafat near Makkah, (5) spending two to three nights at Mina and the symbolic stoning of the devil, and (6) animal sacrifice.

For *hajj* are appointed months. If any one undertakes that duty therein, let there be no obscenity, wickedness, or wrangling in the *hajj* and whatever good you do, (be sure) God knows it. And take a provision (with you) for the journey, but the best of provisions is right conduct. So fear me, O you that are wise! It is not unlawful if you seek of the bounty of your Lord (during pilgrimage). Then when you rush down from (Mount) Arafat, celebrate the praises of God at the Sacred Monument, and celebrate his praises as he has directed you, even though, before this, you went astray. Then pass on at a quick pace from the place whence it is usual for the multitude so to do, and ask for God's forgiveness. For God is oft-forgiving, most merciful. So when you have accomplished your holy rites, celebrate the praises of God, as you used to celebrate the praises of your fathers, yea, with far more heart and soul. There are men who say: Our Lord! Give us (your bounties) in this world! But they will have no portion in the hereafter. And there are men who say: Our Lord! Give us good in this world and good in the hereafter, and protect us from the torment of the fire! To these will be allotted what they have earned; and God is quick in account. Celebrate the praises of God during the appointed days. But if anyone hastens to leave in two days, there is no blame on him, and if anyone stays on, there is no blame on him, if his aim is to do right. Then fear God, and know that you will surely be gathered unto him.

(Baqarah 2:197–203)

Ihram, the first rite of *hajj,* signifies the intention to enter the Sacred House in a state of devotion, as it takes place at specified points, otherwise known as the *miqat,* around the city of Makkah. The pilgrims replace their usual outfits with two pieces of untailored white cloth. From this moment on, all pilgrims enjoy the same simple outfit, the purpose of which is to eliminate social and economic distinctions. Throughout the *hajj* days, pilgrims experience a state of equality with no rank or distinction. In every phase of *hajj,* pilgrims share the same space, perform the same obligations, and stand side by side. So despite their age, race, and ethnic differences, they all experience an amazing state of equality in which no one can appeal to his or her social or economic status or claim special privileges. The only privileged individuals are, paradoxically, the most vulnerable and weak of all, who are driven on wheelchairs by family members or carried on special boards around the *Ka'bah* by hired helpers.

Throughout the days of *hajj,* wherever one looks and moves, one is confronted with a multitude of people who wear the same simple outfit, who constantly declare their submission to God, and who continuously pray for his acceptance, support, and forgiveness. The sense of equality is all-pervasive and remarkable. Quraysh, the dominant tribe in Makkah, succeeded, prior to the revelation of the Qur'an, in bringing the order of rank to the *hajj,* as it insisted that its members stand in a separate site closer to Makkah (Muzdalifah) during the day of Arafat, rather than joining the rest of the visiting pilgrims. The practice was, however, discontinued as the Qur'an made it abundantly clear that Quraysh, like everybody else, must stand on the ninth day of the month of *hajj* (Dhu Alhijjah) on Mount Arafat.

The pilgrim senses an amazing mix of emotions and a total feeling of individuality and singularity wrapped in a feeling of complete togetherness. The congruence in movement and chanting makes one feel that he or she is part of a greater body of believers who share the same commitment to the Divine. The pilgrim, surrounded by complete strangers who simultaneously repeat similar prayers and chants, can still concentrate on the act of worship he or she is engaged in as he or she realizes that everyone else is busy in doing their own rites.

Circumambulating the Sacred House seven times along with countless human beings in a counter-clockwise movement known as *tawaf*, which resembles the movement of celestial bodies throughout the universe, gives the pilgrims the feeling that they are in complete accord not only among themselves, but also with the rest of the creation, in a universal movement that celebrates the glory of God.

As the pilgrims compass round the Sacred House, they repeat the chant that is the hallmark of *hajj*:

> I am here at your service, O God, I am here. I am here, you have no partner, I am here. Indeed, all praise and all blessings and all dominions belong to you. You have no partner.

The circular movement around the Sacred House not only brings the pilgrims into total harmony with one another, but it also brings them into complete harmony with the universe. The counter-clockwise circular movement can be found in the movement of the earth around its axis, as well as in its movement, along with other planets, around the sun. The circular movement of the pilgrims follows, likewise, the same counter-clockwise direction of the solar system, the Milky Way, and all known galaxies throughout the universe. The rest of the *hajj* rituals, including the walk between the Safa and Marwa hills, the stoning of the devil, and the animal sacrifice, are reenactments and reaffirmations of the practices of Ibrahim, Hajar, and Isma'il.

Perhaps the greatest impression the *hajj* leaves on those who are fortunate enough to perform it is the insight it gives into the notion of resurrection on the day of judgment. When a person, at a moment of truth during the *hajj* rites, is standing in the midst of multitudes of other human beings, deprived of the wealth, power, or social status that set him or her apart from other human beings; and when a person is removed of all that he or she cares for and struggles to achieve in life—it is here that the pilgrim feels sincerely and truly that he or she stands alone in front of God, and that he or she is nothing but one of countless people who are somehow gifted with certain privileges that they will one day have to leave behind. It is here, at this very moment of *hajj*, that one who sets out to perform the duty of *hajj* realizes that he or she will ultimately have to return to God, as an individual who has nothing to fall back onto but the relationship he or she has cultivated with the Divine through commitment, service, and devotion.

Ibrahim's journey to Makkah over 3,000 years ago was full of pain and joy—the pain of difficult and taxing travel and the joy of fulfillment and rewards. Likewise, the journey of *hajj* today is a mix of pleasure and pain—the pain of a physically imposing travel and the joy of experiencing intense spirituality few human beings are capable of attaining otherwise. Despite the great advancement in transportation and communication, the journey continues to exact a considerable physical and emotional toll. Yet the journey is equally spiritually rewarding and fulfilling, as one transcends earthly worries, limitations, and concerns as he or she follows in the footsteps of the friend of God, Ibrahim the devout.

PART IV

COMMUNITY PEACE

Peace with other human beings is contingent on achieving inner peace. Achieving inner peace does not, however, automatically lead to social peace. The latter requires further struggle, the aim of which is to translate moral values into social practices. The moral values accepted and embraced by the community must now take the form of social practices and institutions that constitute the common ground on which social actors must stand.

This struggle is the essence of the Qur'anic notion of *jihad*, the ultimate aim of which is to establish social peace, and through it, universal peace.

CHAPTER 16

Integrity

Integrity (*istiqamah*) is an essential moral quality in both the Qur'an and the prophetic tradition. It underscores a serious attitude toward divine demands and unshakable commitment to moral obligations. It is the outer manifestation of the spiritual maturation and moral discipline of a person. Integrity involves the choice to embrace the moral principles outlined by divine revelation in their totality.

The term *"istiqamah"* literally means "straightforwardness." The straight line is the symbol that the Qur'an frequently uses to denote integrity. In the opening chapter (Surah Fatihah) of the Qur'an, which Muslims repeat in every prayer, worshipers ask God to grant them the Straight Path (*al-sirat al-mustaqim*), "the path of those who did not earn the wrath of the Divine, nor those who have gone astray."

The Qur'an urges the faithful to fully and completely commit themselves to the "Straight Path" and to not digress or stray away from it.

> Therefore stand firm on the straight path as you are commanded, you and those who are with you, and transgress not (from the path); for he sees well all that you do.
>
> (Hud 11:112)

Still, the question we are confronted with when we seek to project our lives along the straight path is: what constitutes *istiqamah*, translated here as "integrity"? What are the human qualities that allow certain people to pursuit a life of integrity?

A deep reading of the Qur'anic injunctions show that integrity is a complex notion that combines and connotes three other Qur'anic concepts: sincerity (*ikhlas*), goodness or good character (*khuluq*), and repentance (*tawbah*).

SINCERITY

Sincerity or good will is the most fundamental quality that allow people to live a truthful life, that is, a life in which the individual places the truth—or what he or she honestly believes to be right and true—over and above personal concerns and interests. A sincere person is a person who means what he or she says and is willing to give up his or her short-term comfort and interests for long-term interests and eternal happiness, by privileging what is right and true. A sincere person is one who intends goodness and is always willing to step back and acknowledge his or her mistakes. The acknowledgement of mistakes, which is the fruit of sincerity, is what the Qur'an call repentance.

The believers are frequently commanded in the Qur'an to maintain an attitude of sincerity and to be true to their covenant with God at all costs.

> It is we who have revealed the book to you in truth: so serve God, offering him sincere devotion. To God does belong sincere devotion.
>
> (Zumar 39:3)

> And they have been commanded no more than this: to worship God, offering him sincere devotion, being true (in faith); to establish regular prayer; and to practice regular charity; and that is the religion right and straight.
>
> (Bayyinah 98:5)

The believers are also commanded to be true to their covenant with God and to fulfill their promises and moral duties:

> O you who believe! Do not knowingly betray God and his messenger, and the trust given to you.
>
> (A'raf 7:27)

> Among the believers are men who have been true to their covenant with God: of them are some who have completed their term, while others are still await, but have never wavered.
>
> (Ahzab 33:23)

GOOD CHARACTER

Integrity, being good will, is manifested in the goodness the believers display when interacting with others. It helps the believer to maintain moderation and avoid excesses, and it ensures that religiosity and religious devotion extend beyond the rituals to take on a humane orientation.

> It is not virtue that you turn your faces toward the east or the west, but it is virtue to believe in God and the last day, and the angels, the book, and the messengers. To spend of the substance out of love for him, for your kin, for orphans, for the needy, for those who ask, and for the ransom of slaves; to be steadfast in prayer, and practice regular charity. To fulfill the contracts which you have made, and to be firm and patient in pain, adversity,

and throughout all periods of panic; such are the people of truth, the God-fearing.

(Baqarah 2: 177)

Faith in God, the day of judgment, the angels, the prophets, and the revealed books, is not separate from charity and the willingness to confront injustice, excesses, and oppression. The moral integrity of the believer compels him or her to embrace all moral virtues in all their manifestations and confront corruption in all its forms. Hence, a profound faith is inseparable from good character. A man asked the Prophet about good character; the Prophet recited the *ayah* "Hold to forgiveness, command what is right, and turn away from the ignorant," and then he said: "It is to mend ties with relatives who broke their ties with you, and to give those who withdraw support from you, and to forgive those who exploited you" (Ibn Mardwah).

And because moral practices are the fruits of true and sincere faith, Prophet Muhammad defined his mission as the completion of moral conducts: "I was sent to complete good character" (reported by Bukhari).

Therefore, when Aishah, the Prophet's wife and the person who knew his conduct most intimately, was asked to describe his character, she did not provide a list of ethical principles, but rather she simply described his moral conduct by referring to the moral source that shaped his character:

His character was the Qur'an.

(Reported by Muslim)

Human goodness is at once a spiritual quality, one that must be cultivated through spiritual and moral discipline by following divine revelation and religious teachings, and also a natural capacity, that is innate to humanity. From the Qur'anic viewpoint there is no contradiction between the two, since divine revelation came to affirm, rather than change, the innate nature of human beings—which has in essence spiritual qualities that emanate from the Divine. For this reason, good character is the outer manifestation of the religious quality of *taqwa*, or God-consciousness, which is, again, common to all good people regardless of their religious persuasion. Religious traditions come to polish and further develop the moral choices of people.

The Prophet was once asked: who is the best of people? He said: The persons with most *taqwa*? They said: We have not asked you about this! He said: The best of them prior to Islam is the best of them in Islam, if they understand.

(Bukhari)

Apparently the companions who were curious to know the mark of being a good person were not satisfied with the first explanation. The Prophet's response was exactly the Qur'anic description of the best of people: "The best of you in the eyes of God is one with highest state of *taqwa.*" When they repeated the question, the Prophet provided them with the outer manifestations of *taqwa:* good attitude and good conduct before and after acknowledging the moral teachings of revelation. The above relationship between being conscious of God (*taqwa*) and having good conduct is expressed in the Prophet's response to a person who asked for advice. "A man asked the Prophet: O Prophet of God give me your advice. The Prophet said: Be conscious of God wherever you are, follow bad actions with good deeds, and maintain good character when dealing with people" (reported by Tirmidhi).

It is also interesting that the Prophet joined consciousness of God and goodness with the anticipation that mistakes and shortcomings are bound to occur. The Prophet, therefore, advised the inquirer to repent every time he falls short of the moral demands of good conduct by following bad deeds with good ones.

REPENTANCE

The discussion about sincerity and good conduct leads us to address the important question of moral failings and repentance. The Qur'an is clear that sins, errors, and mistakes are intrinsic to human beings. No human being is beyond reproach, even the faithful:

> When those come to you who believe in our signs, say: Peace be on you; your Lord has inscribed for himself (the rule of) mercy: verily, if any of you did evil in ignorance, and thereafter repented, and amended (his conduct), lo! He is oft-forgiving, most merciful.
>
> (An'am 6:54)

God in his infinite mercy promised to overlook the sins and mistakes of those who realize that they have committed wrong, and who quickly turn back to God and regret their mistakes. Even the most grievous of sins will be forgiven by God if the sinner regrets his or her sins and reaffirms his or her commitment to God and his revealed words.

> Say: O my servants who have transgressed against their souls! Despair not of the mercy of God: for God forgives all sins: for he is oft-forgiving, most merciful.
>
> (Zumar 39:53)

Repentance, it should be stressed here, is not a tactic to which one may resort to sidestep the moral demands of divine revelation, whereby a person repents with the intention to repeat his sinful conduct the next day. Repentance must be sincere with the firm and solemn resolution to steer away from sin.

> And those who, having done something to be ashamed of, or wronged their own souls, earnestly bring God to mind, and ask for forgiveness for their

sins; and who can forgive sins except God? And are never obstinate in persisting knowingly in (the wrong) they have done.

(Al 'Imran 3:135)

God accepts the repentance of those who do evil in ignorance and repent soon afterwards; to them will God turn in mercy: for God is full of knowledge and wisdom. Of no effect is the repentance of those who continue to do evil, until death faces one of them, and he says: Now have I repented indeed; nor of those who die rejecting faith; for them have we prepared a punishment most grievous.

(Nisa' 4:17–18)

Sincerity, good character, and repentance are the ingredients that make moral integrity. They are so essential for moral conduct that morality cannot be sustained for long without them. Without integrity and its basic ingredients, moral qualities and values, such as generosity, courage, and charity, would be reduced to an outward behavior intended for showing off and impressing other people. Without moral integrity (*istiqamah*), morality is reduced into a cost-benefit calculation that would disappear as soon as the cost exceeded the benefit; with it, moral conduct stands on solid ground and a strong foundation.

CHAPTER 17

Humility and Pride

Pride is the foundation of a responsible and positive life, and it is also the source of a contemptuous and exploitative attitude. Pride is a feeling of self-respect and self-worth. Such a feeling is essential for allowing people to assert themselves, and in order to hold their ground and safeguard their values and beliefs in the face of adversity and through difficult times. Pride could, however, prompt people to commit excesses and prevent them from admitting mistakes and rectifying errors.

If pride is the basis of both socially responsible and socially excessive conducts, the question arises as to how the same quality may produce diametrically opposed responses. Why does self-pride, on the one hand, make certain people committed to moral principles and motivated to do their work in the best possible way, and yet it drives still others to commit excesses and to place their self interests above the wellbeing and dignity of others? The answer to this question lies in the overall character of the proud person.

Pride as self-respect is an attitude that manifests itself in connection to a host of values that define the character of a person. Self-respect associated with the values of faithfulness, compassion, justice, wisdom, and honesty would only lead to moral perfection and an attitude of respect for the dignity of others. However, when self-respect is associated with a self-centered person who fails to develop moral discipline, the person may find it easy to violate the rights and dignity of others in pursuit of one's self-interest. For moral discipline helps people to base their actions on universal values and provides them with a sense of social responsibility that transcends the power that one is able to exert on others. A morally disciplined person recognizes that his will must be subordinated to a fair and sublime transcendental will, to a universally equitable law, that is. A person who refuses to submit to a universal law, and who sees his individual will as paramount, would be only restrained by the extent of his power.

Self-pride associated with moral discipline and the recognition of human limitations, along with the imperative to submit to a higher will and higher law, produces an attitude of humility and respect of human dignity, while self-pride deprived of these qualities can only result in excessive and arrogant behavior.

Self-pride as arrogance manifested itself first in the response of Iblis (Lucifer) to the Divine's command to bow down to Adam, the first human being. Iblis refused to bow down. When God asked him to explain his rebellion in the face of the divine command, his response was illuminating and instructive.

> O Iblis what prevents you from prostrating yourself to one whom I have created with my hands, are you haughty? Or are you one of the highest? (Iblis) said: I am better than he: you created me from fire and him you created from clay.
>
> (Sad 38:72–76)

"I am better than he," Iblis reasoned. Like human beings, Iblis was a finite being, with limited rationality and knowledge, and hence he was not in a position to pass judgment on purposes and events that transcended his knowledge and reason. He should have recognized that the command given to him, by the one who created him as well as Adam, was intended as a gesture to acknowledge the superior mission human beings are entrusted with. However, rather than recognizing the limitations of his knowledge and judgment and the superiority of the knowledge and the will that commanded him, he turned to his physical attributes and judged that his were superior over Adam's, and he thought that his self-perception was sufficient to invalidate the divine command: "I am better than he; you created me from fire and created him from clay."

Iblis's arrogance, ignorance, and even racism are hard to miss. Fire is better than clay, he reasoned, so he was better than Adam, he concluded. It is not difficult to see the flawed reasoning of Iblis in assuming that comparison should be limited to physical attributes. He should have further recognized that such an assertion, while easy to refute in theory, has been historically shown to be absolutely erroneous. For not only did Adam possess creative spirituality that eluded Iblis's, even the angels', judgment, but Adam's physical qualities were not sufficiently appreciated. The physical qualities of humans gave them the drive and incentive to transform their physical environment in ways that would not have been possible otherwise. The fact that they were made of clay and shared the physical density and inertia associated with organic substance gave them the incentive to transform the natural order, and it empowered them to translate their ideas and thoughts into objects, tools, and artifacts. It is, obviously, sheer arrogance, rather than knowledge, that prompted Iblis to declare his superiority. And arrogance was evidently the ground for the first sin in the history of the universe, and it continues to be the ground for justifying injustice in human societies.

In posing the rhetorical question to Iblis that was intended to help him examine his rebellious attitude, God put the issue in astounding clarity: "What prevents you from prostrating yourself to one whom I have created with my hands, are you haughty or are you one of the highest?" Iblis's disgraceful response could rest on one of two grounds: either he was higher than the Divine in wisdom, knowledge, and foresight—which he was obviously not—or he was simply an arrogant person.

Iblis had the chance at this point to retreat and to acknowledge his mistake, but he was, alas, stubborn, and he set out on a mission to justify his arrogance. Instead of repenting and acknowledging his foolish mistake, he asked for a respite to prove that humanity is not worthy of the dignity and importance assigned to it.

> He said: Give me respite till the day they are raised up. (God) said: Be you amongst those who have respite. He said: Because you have thrown me out of the way, lo! I will lie in wait for them on your straight way: Then will I approach them from before them and behind them, from their right and their left: nor will you find, in most of them, gratitude (for your mercies).
>
> (A'raf 7:14–17)

Iblis, it turned out, was not the only haughty being, as he succeeded in finding followers and supporters from within the human race. One such person that the Qur'an uses as an example of arrogant humanity was Pharaoh, the tyrant of ancient Egypt. Like Satan, Pharaoh was a self-centered being, who elevated his will over and above the universal law of the divine will. And like Iblis, Pharaoh relied on the physical attributes of race to elevate certain people and put down others.

> Truly Pharaoh elated himself in the land and broke up its people into sections, depressing a small group among them: their sons he slew, but he kept alive their females: for he was indeed a maker of mischief.
>
> (Qasas 28:4)

The "I am better than he," has now taken the form of "we are better than they," the usual mantra of the arrogant and the racist. "We are better than they" has always been the foundation of abuse and injustice, through which a racial, ethnic, or religious community could elevate itself over and above other human communities and could then indulge itself in the worst abuse and exploitation human beings are capable of inflicting on one another.

ARROGANCE BREEDS IGNORANCE

When self-pride is deprived of faith and wisdom, it turns to arrogance that prevents a person from submitting to the rules of transcendental law. Utmost among the rules of universal law is that all people share equal human dignity, and that all have equal claims to justice, fairness, and equity. The haughty is so self-centered that he or she is unable to recognize the universal law of justice and equity demanded by the Divine.

Arrogance, the Qur'an asserts, has always been the main obstacle preventing people from recognizing the truth:

> When it is said to him: Fear God, he is led by arrogance to (more) crime. Enough for him is hell; an evil bed indeed (to lie on)!
>
> (Baqarah 2:206)

It is not that truth, right, and justice are difficult to discern, for the unfaithful do discern it deep in their hearts, but rather it is that their false pride and contempt of those who are less fortunate drive them to stubbornly deny what they have already discerned:

> And they rejected those signs in iniquity and arrogance, though their souls were convinced thereof: so consider the end of the corrupt!
>
> (Naml 27:14)

Rather than being grateful to God for providing them with wealth and power, the corrupt often reject the truth brought to them by their prophets, pointing out that they cannot accept the revelation that equates them in dignity with the less fortunate members of the community.

> They said: Shall we believe in you when it is the least among us that follow you? He said: And what do I know as to what they do? Their account is only with my Lord, if you could (but) understand. I am not one to drive away those who believe. I am sent only to warn plainly in public.
>
> (Shu'ara 26:111–115)

Not only does arrogance drive people to look with contempt at people who have little means, but it also lures them to moral decadence, notably to envy and jealousy.

> But the chiefs of the unbelievers among his people said: We see (in) you nothing but a man like ourselves: nor do we see that any follow you but the meanest among us, in judgment immature: nor do we see in you (all) any merit above us: in fact we think you are liars!
>
> (Hud 11:27)

It is arrogance that prevents the haughty from accepting revealed truth, because revelation does not discriminate between the wealthy and the poor and the powerful and weak, but rather it always insists that the wealthy and powerful must show compassion towards, and take responsibility for improving the social conditions of, the least fortunate.

> Is it that whenever there comes to you a messenger with what you yourselves desire not, you are puffed up with pride? Some you call impostors and others you slay.
>
> (Baqarah 2:87)

Those who dispute about the signs of God without any authority bestowed on them—there is nothing in their hearts but (the quest for) greatness which they shall never attain.

(Ghafir 40:56)

Grievous and odious, in the sight of God and of the believers, is the conduct of those who dispute about the signs of God without any authority that has reached them. Thus does God seal up every heart of arrogant and overpowering.

(Ghafir 40:35)

ARROGANCE BREEDS TYRANNY AND CORRUPTION

Nothing corrupts a person more than the feeling that the power and wealth he enjoys are of his own making and that, because of that, he is more deserving than other human beings. Indeed, it is very easy for humans to delude themselves as they compare their power and wealth with those who are deprived of them. Power and wealth, deprived of faith and wisdom, corrupt those who possess them.

To illustrate this point, the Qur'an narrates the story of Qarun (or Korah son of Izhar in the Bible), a contemporary of Musa (Moses) who was endowed with great wealth, but who failed to recognize that his wealth was his opportunity to make a positive impact on his community and improve the human condition.

> Qarun was, undoubtedly, of the people of Musa; but he acted insolently towards them: such were the treasures we had bestowed on him, that their very keys would have been a burden to a body of strong men. Behold, his people said to him: Exult not, for God loves not those who exult (in riches). But seek, with the (wealth) which God has bestowed on you, the home of the hereafter, nor forget your portion in this world: but do good, as God has been good to you, and seek not (occasions for) mischief in the land: for God loves not those who do mischief. He said: This has been given to me because of a certain knowledge which I have. Did he not know that God had destroyed, before him (whole) generations—which were superior to him in strength and greater in amount (of riches) they had collected? But the wicked are not called (immediately) to account for their sins. So he went forth among his people in the (pride of his worldly) glitter. Said those whose aim is the life of this world: Oh! That we had the like of what Qarun has got! For he is truly a lord of mighty good fortune! But those who had been granted (true) knowledge said: Alas for you! The reward of God (in the here-after) is best for those who believe and work righteousness: but this none shall attain, save those who steadfastly persevere (in good). Then we caused the earth to swallow him up and his dwelling place; and he had not (the least little) party to help him against God, nor could he defend himself. And those who had envied his position the day before began to say on the morrow: Ah! It is indeed God who enlarges the provision or restricts it,

to any of his servants he pleases! Had it not been that God was gracious to
us, he could have caused the earth to swallow us up! Ah! Those who reject
God will assuredly never prosper. That house of the hereafter we shall give
to those who intend not exultation or mischief on earth: and the end is (best)
for the righteous.

(Qasas 28:76–83)

Qarun ultimately perished with his wealth, leaving behind nothing
that can be recounted as a contribution to human life, except the pity that
was felt by those who were once his admirers. A person who wastes life
opportunities and resources because he is consumed by arrogance may
well deserve all the pity that he or she can get.

The right attitude of a person who is endowed with wealth and power
should never be a sense of false pride but rather a sense of responsibility,
even when his wealth and power are achieved through diligence and
hard work. For one must realize that the circumstances and opportunities
that are vital for any human being to progress in life are never of his own
making, but rather they are external factors provided for a purpose. The
Qur'an is clear in associating levels of human capacity with the overall
mission of humanity, on the one hand, and to the individual's trials of life,
on the other.

It is he who has made you (his) agents, inheritors of the earth: he has raised
some of you in ranks over others: that he may try you in the gift he has given
you.

(An'am 6:165)

Arrogance does not only waste energy and resources but also leads to
tyranny and injustice. The story of Pharaoh illustrates this dimension of
self-pride that has not been nurtured through faith and humility and
has hence degenerated into arrogance and aggression. Pharaoh misread
the extraordinary power he enjoyed as the head of a powerful nation
endowed with great resources. He saw his power as a sign of his intrinsic greatness, and it did not, therefore, take long before his sense of self
was inflated. He elevated himself above all humans and surrounded
himself with corrupt people who bought their position of privilege
though lavish praise and self-denigration. Surrounded by a hero-
worshiping cult, he was deprived of the advice of wise men and experienced people.

With delusional and corrupt political elites surrounding him, it was
only a matter of time before the power of Pharaoh was used to exploit
people and corrupt society. Such elites are bound to perpetuate their delu-
sions by suppressing knowledge and silencing those who advocate right
and justice. Not only did he enslave the Israelites, who lived in Egypt
along the native Egyptians, he also used force to impose his false beliefs
on the people:

But none believed in Musa except some children of his people, because of the
fear of Pharaoh and his chiefs, lest they should persecute them; and certainly
Pharaoh was mighty on the earth and one who transgressed all bounds.

(Yunus 10:83)

Arrogance leads to crimes, as the arrogant who elevates himself above
others likewise elevates himself above the law. Unrestrained by a universal
law, the arrogant indulge in exploitation and excess.

As to those who rejected God, (to them will be said): Were not our signs
rehearsed to you? But you were arrogant and were a people given to crime!

(Jathiyah 45:31)

And when you exert your strong hands (against opponents), you do it as
if you have an absolute power.

(Shu'ara 26:150)

TRUE PRIDE ROOTED IN FAITH

Self pride rooted in faith is a powerful force, because it creates a strong
attachment to one's values and standards and dislike to falling below these
standards. And because it is based on the principles of the transcendental
law, it is rooted in the divine will and emanates from the glory of the Divine.

If any do seek for glory and power, to God belong all glory and power.
To him mount up (all) words of purity: it is he who exalts each deed of righteousness. Those that lay plots of evil, for them is a penalty terrible; and the
plotting of such will be void (of result).

(Fatir 35: 10)

Those who seek glory in lies, deception, injustice, and exploitation
are delusional, and they soon realize that all glory belongs to God and
to those who are true to the sublime principles and values associated
with him.

They say: If we return to Medina, surely the more honorable (element) will
expel therefrom the meaner. But honor belongs to God and his messenger,
and to the believers; but the hypocrites know not.

(Yasin 36:8)

The faithful may experience challenging circumstances and times,
whereby the forces of injustice and corruption might appear to have the
upper hand. But the faithful should never feel discouraged and subdued,
as values and beliefs they stand for are bound to triumph, as they always
have throughout human history. The trying times they experience must
always be viewed as trying times, an opportunity to prove their commitment, a time of moral and spiritual elevation and growth.

So lose not heart, nor fall into despair: for you must gain mastery if you are
true in faith. If a wound has touched you, be sure a similar wound has

touched the others. Such days (of varying fortunes) we give to people and people by turns: that God may know those that believe, and that he may take to himself from your ranks martyr-witnesses (to truth). And God loves not those that do wrong. God's object also is to purge those that are true in faith and to deprive of blessing those that resist faith. Did you think that you would enter heaven without God testing those of you who fought hard (in his cause) and remained steadfast?

(Al 'Imran 3:139–142)

HUMILITY

Self-pride rooted in deep faith is a pride that is always aware of human limitations and the grace and blessings of God. It is pride constrained with humility and gratitude, and hence it has a desire to express that gratitude in ways that please God, improve the human condition, and uplift the human spirit. It is the pride of the strong who knows that his or her strength is a gift of God that can be taken away in a split second, and hence who wants to use his strength to leave a positive legacy. And it is the pride of the wise who know well that respect is generated through humility, and leadership through service.

And swell not your cheek (for pride) at men, nor walk in insolence through the earth: for God loves not any arrogant boaster.

(Luqman 31:44)

...but lower your wing (in gentleness) to the believers.

(Hijr 15:88)

And it is the pride of the person who gets satisfaction and gratification from achieving and not simply from being, who thus is focused on completing the mission with perfection and success, rather than enjoying the ride. This was the self-pride of Musa (Moses) and Harun (Aaron), who displayed great self-confidence as they embarked on their difficult mission and followed divine instructions in using courtesy and good manners even when approaching the tyrant of Egypt. They well realized that their mission was not to humiliate the tyrant but to free the children of Israel.

But speak to him mildly; perchance he may take warning or fear (God).

(Taha 20:44)

It is the same humility that was displayed by all the prophets, as they approached people who they well knew were misguided. They nevertheless treated such people with the utmost respect and showed great humility while engaging them.

Say: You shall not be questioned as to our sins, nor shall we be questioned as to what you do.

(Saba' 34:26)

Prophet Muhammad, likewise, was praised for his kindness and humility toward those whom he was sent to guide. He was further instructed to overlook the shortcomings of his followers and to consult with them in public matters.

> It is part of the mercy of God that you do deal gently with them. Were you severe or harsh-hearted, they would have broken away from about you: so pass over (their faults), and ask for (God's) forgiveness for them; and consult them in affairs (of moment). Then, when you have taken a decision, put your trust in God, for God loves those who put their trust (in him).
>
> (Al 'Imran 3:159)

Not only does the Qur'an reject viewing other human beings with contempt, but it also opposes the use of force for advancing revealed values and beliefs.

> We know best what they say; and you are not one to overawe them by force. So admonish with the Qur'an such as fear my warning!
>
> (Qaf 50:45)

Being humble, kind, and forbearing does not mean that one should be soft in the face of individuals and groups who are given to corruption and injustice. The same humble believers are expected to take a firm and strong stand in the face of tyranny and injustice.

The Prophet underscored the basic elements of arrogance when he realized that some of his companions were confused over who it was that could be called arrogant. In a *hadith* that was reported by Imam Muslim on the authority of Ibn Masud, he stated:

> No person with an aught of arrogance shall enter into paradise. A man said: Everyone likes to have good outfits and good shoes. He said: God is beauty and loves beauty. Arrogance lies in denying what is right and looking down on people.

CHAPTER 18

Moderation and Excess

Moderation is considered a virtue in both ancient philosophy and revealed religions. Greek philosophers regarded moderation as one of four fundamental moral virtues. All established religious and philosophical traditions urge followers to exercise moderation in views and practices and to avoid extravagance and excesses.

Moderation is central to the moral discipline emphasized by the Qur'an. The Qur'an directs Muslims to seek moderation in religious practices and spending, and it warns them against fanaticism and extravagance. The Prophet of Islam, likewise, warned Muslims not to commit excesses, and he took every occasion to remind them to be moderate. "Seek religious duties with care and avoid haste," he stressed, "for the hasty often fails to complete his journey and destroys the vessel that carries him" (Ibn Hiban).

UNIVERSAL BALANCE AND OPEN POSSIBILITIES

Moderation has always been an important virtue, but it is becoming exceedingly more important as we witness the rise of extremist voices of every religious community, that are working hard to drive our world out of balance. Extreme voices on all sides are full of rage and hate, and they are stirring emotions and clouding people's understanding and vision.

A moderate person is one who seeks a balanced life, who avoids extreme religious and social views and practices, as he or she steers away from excessive behavior and extravagant life.

Balance is an important universal principle, essential, the Qur'an stresses, for both the natural and human orders.

> And the heaven has he raised high, and he has set up the balance (of justice), in order that you may not transgress (due) balance. So establish weight with justice and fall not short in the balance.
>
> (Rahman 55:7–9)

As the universe has been created with great precision, whereby various objects and forces balance one another in complete harmony, so should balance and moderation be maintained in human society to ensure social harmony and justice. Individual moderation and social harmony are, therefore, the basic goals of the Islamic revelation.

> Thus, have we made of you a community (*ummah*) justly balanced, that you might be witnesses over the peoples, and the messenger a witness over yourselves.
>
> (Baqarah 2:143)

The Muslim community is expected, the Qur'an tells us, to set high moral standards to the rest of humanity, as the Prophet set an example of exemplary character and moral conduct to the community of believers he established.

To do that, Muslims are expected to develop moral discipline, by constantly choosing right and justice over self-indulgence and corruption. Human nature is open to the possibilities of both good and evil, morality and corruption, and gratitude and ingratitude.

> Verily we created man from a drop of mingled sperm in order to try him: so we gave him (the gift) of hearing and sight. We showed him the way: whether he be grateful or ungrateful.
>
> (Dahr 76:2–3)

Life consists of a series of tests and challenges that try human beings to the deepest recesses of their souls. The trials of life take the form of the choices people make, day in and day out, that contribute to either the enrichment of human life or its degradation.

> By the soul and the proportion and order given to it, and its enlightenment as to its wrong and its right: truly he succeeds that purifies it, and fails that corrupts it.
>
> (Shams 91:7–10)

Perhaps the most important choice humans make is to recognize their humanness: to recognize, that is, the human condition and to realize that people are neither absolute beings in full control of the complex human world, nor helpless creatures that have no effect on developing the social and natural orders. All human miseries and injustices result from ignoring human limitations and from exceeding the moral and intellectual boundaries associated with a mortal and transient humanity.

MORAL DEFICIENCIES BREED SOCIAL EXCESSES

Those who fail to recognize their human essence harbor distorted beliefs and are likely to commit excesses. Distortion in belief leads to injustice and excess, as would injustice and excess lead to distortion of belief. Hence we see that the Qur'an always associates excess (*israf*) with a rebellious attitude toward God. *Israf* occurs when people go beyond human limitations, and this exactly is what rebellion against God is all about. Both distortion and excess are an aberration of human life; though one is mental and the other is practical, both denote the same type of existence. One happens through perception; the other through words and actions.

It is this combination of distortion and excess that one finds in the Qur'anic indictment and condemnation of Pharaoh:

> Indeed Pharaoh was haughty on the earth and one who transgressed all bound.
>
> (Yunus 10:83)

Pharaoh's excessive behavior, manifested in the exploitation and abuse of the Israelites, including killing their infant boys for fear that one of them would challenge him, was rooted, the above verse points out, in his condescending attitude towards others. The Qur'anic message is crystal clear:*the sins of the hand and the tongue are rooted in the sins of the heart.* To ensure that one does not overstep his or her boundaries and indulge in exploitation, injustice, and aggression, one must develop moral discipline to avoid social excesses. A person with a deep sense of equality and deep respect for human life and dignity is unlikely to commit aggressive acts and indulge in exploitation.

For excess to take place in society, a deficiency must already be force. No excess is possible without deficiency, as no master can exist without a slave. Deficiency is the other side of excess, and slavery is other side of tyranny. To stop social excess we must overcome moral deficiency, and to prevent slavery we must nurture a culture of equal freedom and dignity.

> Thus did he make fools of his people, and they obeyed him: truly were they a people rebellious (against God).
>
> (Zukhruf 43:54)

Pharaoh's excesses were possible because of the moral deficiencies of his people, who allowed him, through their complacency, to make fools of them as he extended his authority and power beyond what humans may and should claim.

Divine revelation warns against spiritual deficiencies and social excesses, seeing in one the path to the other. When the human spirit is not nurtured, the human being is prone to indulge in social excesses, including violating human life, abusing helpless people, and appropriating the work and resources of others. Killing, insulting, defaming, stealing, and robbing are all grave violations of the divine covenants and are major sins. But the greatest violation, the greatest sin of all, lies in an attitude that many people would not consider harmful: arrogance.

FAILING TO RECOGNIZE HUMAN LIMITS

Excess takes many forms, all of which involve actions that exceed the limitations placed on humans by the Divine. Excess is not simply engaging in a specific type of behavior but engaging in it in ways that defy transcendental principles and purposes. Human life is, for example, considered sacred and may not be violated by other human beings. Its violation is a great sin and a crime against the entire human race, unless it is done as retribution for another life or for penalizing the violation of public security and social peace.

> On that account [of Cain killing Abel]: We ordained for the children of Israel that if anyone slew a person—unless it be for murder or for spreading mischief in the land—it would be as if he slew the whole people: and if any one saved a life, it would be as if he saved the life of the whole people. Then although there came to them our messengers with clear signs, yet, even after that, many of them continued to commit excesses in the land.
>
> (Ma'idah 5: 32)

To engage in excesses is to go beyond the bounds set by God and enshrined in the human spirit. It is to focus on one important thing while neglecting equally important others. And it is to pick and choose and to indulge in self-gratification, while ignoring the demands of right and justice.

Avoiding excesses does not mean, therefore, that one should engage in self–denial but that one should seek moderation. It is not deficiency that constrains human excess, but rather moderation. Put more clearly, the Qur'an sees both deficiencies and excesses as aberrations and moral perversion. To be morally and spiritually upright is to choose moderation. The Qur'an does not require Muslims to give up beautiful outfits, or to deny themselves the joy of delicious food and beverages, but rather to avoid excessive and unrestrained consumption. It requires moderation.

> O children of Adam! Wear your beautiful apparel at every time and place of prayer: eat and drink: but waste not by excess, for God loves not the wasters.
>
> (A'raf 7:31)

Likewise, the Qur'an does not oppose the creation of wealth and the enjoyment of property as long as proprietors contribute part of their wealth to the less fortunate.

> Eat of its fruit when it bears fruit, and pay the due of it on the day of its reaping, and do not act extravagantly; surely he does not love the extravagant.
>
> (An'am 6:141)

Recognizing human limitations requires that, in making decision and choices, one has to steer away from the extremes and seek a middle ground.

SPIRITUAL MODERATION

Choosing moderation and steering away from extremism is not only demanded in the realm of material enjoyment but also in religious practices and worship. The Qur'an counsels to use moderation in the application of religious practices and warns against excesses in matters of religion.

> Say: O People of the Book! exceed not in your religion the bounds (of what is proper), trespassing beyond the truth, nor follow the vain desires of people who went wrong in times gone by, who misled many, and strayed (themselves) from the even way.
>
> (Ma'idah 5:77)

The Qur'an does not see a life of complete devotion to spirituality as an exemplary life, but rather as an individual choice. While the Qur'an tolerates the life of monasticism, it sees in it the potential for excess:

> Then, in their wake, we followed them up with (others of) our messengers: we sent after them 'Isa (Jesus) the son of Maryam (Mary), and bestowed on him the gospel; and we ordained in the hearts of those who followed him compassion and mercy, but the monasticism which they invented for themselves, we did not prescribe for them: (we commanded) only the seeking for the good pleasure of God; but that they did not foster as they should have done. Yet we bestowed, on those among them who believed, their (due) reward, but many of them are rebellious transgressors.
>
> (Hadid 57: 27)

The Prophet reiterated and clarified the Qur'anic position regarding the undesirability of a life of complete spiritual devotion:

> Bukhari and Muslim reported on the authority of Anas, may God be pleased with him, who said: Three persons went to the Prophet's wives and asked them about his worship. When they were told, they felt he did not do enough, and then said: Who are we of the Prophet, peace be with him; he was forgiven his past and future sins! One of them said: I will pray throughout the night and will never rest; the second said: I will fast every day and will never break my daily fast; the third person said: I will stay celibate and will never get married. The Prophet came to them and said: Did you say that? By God I am the most fearful of God and the most devout among you; but I fast [on days] and eat [on others]; pray [part of the night] and rest; and I do marry; who ever choose a different tradition he is not of me.

Clearly, the Prophet abhorred excess even in worship and spoke against it in very strong terms. He indeed cautioned the believers against being hasty and tense in pursuing religious duties. Bukhari reported the following prophetic statement:

> Seek religious duties with care and avoid haste, and do not overburden yourselves in the worship of God; for the hasty often fails to complete his journey and destroys the vessel that carries him.

The principle that one should not take on responsibilities beyond one's ability to deliver and sustain is repeatedly emphasized in Qur'anic teachings and the prophetic statements:

> On no soul does God place a burden greater than it can bear. It gets every good that it earns, and it suffers every ill that it earns. (Pray:) Our Lord! Condemn us not if we forget or fall into error; our Lord! Lay not on us a burden like that which you did lay on those before us; our Lord! Lay not on us a burden greater than we have strength to bear. Blot out our sins, and grant us forgiveness. Have mercy on us. You are our protector; help us against those who stand against faith.
>
> (Baqarah 2:286)

Bukhari and Muslim reported that the Prophet said:

> Focus on your goal and try your best, and know that no one will enter paradise merely through his own deeds, and that the best of deeds are those that endure even if they were of little significance.

CHOOSING THE MIDDLE WAY

Seeking moderation and maintaining balance often means seeking the middle way and giving equal weight to the different demands placed on us. Moderation requires that one should neither neglect a need or a duty, nor become completely occupied with a particular need or duty.

In matters of spending, moderation means to avoid overspending or underspending but to seek instead a middle position. Spending must be purposive and proportionate.

> Make not your hand tied (like a niggard's) to your neck, nor stretch it forth to its utmost reach, so that you become blameworthy and destitute.
>
> (Isra' 17:29)

> And they [the servants of God] are those who when they spend, are neither extravagant nor parsimonious, and (keep) between these the just mean.
>
> (Furqan 25:67)

And in matters of communication and expression, one should seek the middle way and be purposive and proportionate:

> And be moderate in your pace, and lower your voice; for the harshest of sounds without doubt is the braying of the donkey.
>
> (Luqman 31:19)

When, therefore, people find themselves in a position of abundance, influence, and power—away from the middle—they are morally required to find their way back to the balanced middle rather than indulge in a life of extravagance. It is their moral obligation and religious duty to use their wealth and power in ways that will bring good to the life of others and help those in need. In failing to do that, they would be guilty of excess.

Why were there not, among the generations before you, persons possessed of balanced good sense, prohibiting (men) from mischief in the earth—except a few among them whom we saved (from harm)? But the wrongdoers pursued the enjoyment of the good things of life which were given them, and persisted in sin.

(Hud 11:116)

Moderation is clearly the outward expression of the inner state of integrity and balance. Like moral integrity, moderation is closely linked with the important Qur'anic concept of the "Straight Path." For moderation, deep inside, relates to unceasing efforts to keep one's eyes on the purpose of life and action, and that one never indulge in aimless and harmful talk and action. It is about keeping eyes on the goal and choosing the surest path, the straight path, and never wondering aimlessly or taking a tangent that could take one away from the route to the desired end. Moderation is about avoiding a life of extremes, even when the intention is pursuing matters deemed to be of goodness and piety. This is because an extreme position cannot be maintained for long and could possibly disorient the road traveler and thorw him or her out of the right trajectory, or it could lead to fatigue and exhaustion that might force the exhausted person to give up the goal and mission all together.

CHAPTER 19

Jihad for Peace

The Qur'an has a vision of peace and demands strict observance of the values necessary for bringing about a peaceful world. It teaches Muslims to submit and surrender their individual wills to a higher truth and a transcendental law, so that one can lead a meaningful life informed by the divine purpose of creation, where the dignity and freedom of all human beings can be equally protected. Islamic teachings assert the basic freedom and equality of all peoples. The Qur'an stresses the importance of mutual help and respect, and it directs Muslims to extend friendship and good will to all, regardless of their religious, ethnic, or racial background.

ISLAM'S VISION OF PEACE

A systematic examination of Islamic texts and Muslim history shows that peace is, and has always been, the original position and final aim of Islam. War can and must be fought, however, to repel aggression and lift oppression—but only as the last resort. War should not be seen as an instrument for advancing ideological commitments of the bearers of political power. War is not, and should never be, a political choice. War in Islam has specific objectives, and these objectives revolve around defending human dignity. Advancing narrow interests and imposing religious beliefs are not legitimate objectives of war in Islam.

From its inception, the Qur'an has emphasized peace as an intrinsic Islamic value. In fact, the terms "Islam" and "*salam*," or peace, have the same Arabic root, "slm." Furthermore, God has chosen the word "peace" (*salam*) as the Muslim's greeting. Reviewing early Muslim history and reflecting on the experience of the early Muslim generations, one can clearly see that peace was always the original position of Muslims, and that war was either a punitive measure to annihilate tyranny and oppression or a defensive measure to stop aggression. From the very beginning,

Prophet Muhammad was instructed to use a friendly and polite approach to call people to Islam.

> Invite (all) to the way of your Lord with wisdom and beautiful preaching; and argue with them in ways that are best and most gracious: for your Lord knows best, who have strayed from his path, and who receive guidance.
>
> (Nahl 16:125)

Although the Qur'an often uses the word *"jihad"* in reference to the act of war, it gives the term broader meaning. The term *"jihad"* was first introduced in the Makkan Qur'an long before the Muslims were permitted to fight. In the Makkan period, the term was used in reference to peaceful struggle in the way of God:

> And those who strive (make jihad) in our way, we will certainly guide them to our paths: for verily God is with those who do right.
>
> ('Ankabut 29:69)

> Therefore listen not to the unbelievers, but strive against them with the utmost strenuousness, with the Qur'an.
>
> (Furqan 25:52)

These Qur'anic verses direct early Muslims to patiently persevere in the face of Quraysh's persecution and oppression and to rely on dialogue and communication to establish just peace. It follows that fighting and using military tactics is only one of several avenues through which the duty of *jihad* can be discharged. *Jihad* includes, in addition to military struggle, peaceful resistance against tyranny and political struggle for ensuring accountability and fair governance.

The Qur'an urges Muslims to seek a political order based on peaceful cooperation and mutual respect, and it warns them against placing religious solidarity over covenanted rights and the principles of justice:

> Those who believed, and migrated, and fought for the faith with their property and their persons, in the cause of God, as well as those who gave (them) asylum and aid—these are (all) friends and protectors, one of another. As to those who believed but chose not to migrate, you owe no duty of protection to them until they migrate; but if they seek your aid in religion, it is your duty to help them, except against a people with whom you have a treaty of mutual alliance. And (remember) God sees all that you do. The unbelievers are protectors, one of another: unless you do this (protect each other), there would be oppression and commotion on earth, and great mischief.
>
> (Anfal 8: 72)

The Qur'an, therefore, directs Muslims to find a common ground with other religious communities. This common ground is expressed as a mutual respect of the freedom and autonomy of different religious communities.

> To each among you have we prescribed a law and an open way. If God had so willed he would have made you a single people, but (his plan is) to test you in what he has given you: so strive as in a race in all virtues. The goal of you all is to God: it is he that will show you the truth of the matters in which you dispute.
>
> (Ma'idah 5:48)

No religious community, the Qur'an stresses, should appropriate to itself the right to impose its way of life on other religious communities. The Qur'an is also clear that there can be no force in matters religious.

> Let there be no compulsion in religion: truth stands out clear from error.
>
> (Baqarah 2: 256)

> If it had been the Lord's will, they would all have believed—all who are on earth! Will you then compel mankind against their will to believe?
>
> (Yunus 10: 98)

Still, peace in Islam does not merely mean the absence of war but the absence of oppression and tyranny as well. Islam considers that real peace can only be attained when justice prevails. Islam, therefore, justifies war against regimes that prevent people from choosing their ideals and practicing their beliefs. It does not, however, justify war against non-Muslim entities that neither prevent the peaceful practicing of Islam nor inflict wrong upon Muslims.

ARMED *JIHAD*

Islam permits its followers to resort to armed struggle to repel military aggression, and indeed it urges them to fight oppression, brutality, and injustice. The Qur'anic term for such a struggle is *jihad*. Yet for many in the West, *jihad* is nothing more than a holy war, that is, a war to force one's religious beliefs on others. Most Muslims would reject the equation of *jihad* with holy war, and they would insist that a better description, one that captures the essence of the Islamic concept of *jihad*, is that of just war. There are still fringe groups who conceive *jihad* as a divine license to use violence to impose their will on anyone they can brand as an infidel, including fellow Muslims who may not fit their self-proclaimed categorization of right and wrong.

The confusion about the meaning of *jihad*, and the debate over whether *jihad* is a "holy war" or a "just war" is of great importance for Muslims and non-Muslims alike, particularly at this juncture of human history, when the world has once again rejected narrow nationalist politics and is moving rapidly to embrace the notion of global peace and the notion of a multicultural and multireligious society.

Thus it is very crucial to expose the confusion of those who insist that *jihad* is a holy war and who place doubts on Islam's ability to support global peace. The advocates of *jihad* as a holy war constitute today a tiny minority of intellectuals in both Muslim societies and the West. Western scholars who accept *jihad* as a holy war feed on the position of radical Muslim ideologues, as well as on generalization from the particular and exceptional to the general.

The aim of war, the Qur'an stresses, is not to propagate or spread Islam, nor is it to expand the territory of the Islamic state or to dominate, politically or militarily, non-Muslim regions. Rather, the aim of war is to establish and ensure just peace, as well as to annihilate oppression and abolish tyranny. It is true that the right to communicate the message of Islam is protected under Islamic law, and the Islamic state must, therefore, respect and defend this right. But the obligation to protect the right of Muslims, and for this matter all religious communities, to practice their beliefs and values should be carried out through peaceful means and in a friendly manner.

We can identify four limits on the use of military force; the first two relate to the purpose of war, while the remaining two relate to the conduct of war.

PURPOSE OF WAR

There are two, and only two, reasons that justify armed *jihad:* (1) reciprocity and the right to repel violence with violence, and (2) war against oppression.

1. Reciprocity and the Right to Repel Violence with Violence

Returning violence for violence is an established right for any political community which has been the target of military aggression. The Qur'an states: "Fight in the cause of God those who fight you, but do not transgress limits; for God loves not transgressors" (Baqarah 2:190).

Reciprocity also requires that when the enemy elects to cease hostility and end the conflict, Muslims are under obligation to seek peace and forgo war: "And if they incline to peace, you too should incline to peace, and put your trust in God. Surely God is all hearing and all knowing. If they seek to deceive you, behold, God is enough for you" (Anfal 8:61).

This interpretation was upheld by classical Muslim scholars. Ibn Taymiyah, for instance, concluded that since God has permitted the taking of life only insofar as it is necessary to protect against greater evil of widespread injustice and turmoil: "...any (unbeliever) who does not prevent Muslims from practicing the religion of God, he hurts by his disbelief no one but his own soul."

2. War against Oppression

It is incumbent upon Muslims to challenge any political authority that either uses its power to impose a particular set of religious views and beliefs, or that prevents people from freely professing or practicing the religion they chose to embrace.

And fight them until there is no more persecution and religion is only for God.

(Baqarah 2:193)

And why should you not fight in the cause of God and of those who, being weak, are oppressed—men, women, and children, whose cry is: Our Lord, rescue us from this town, whose people are oppressors; and raise for us from you one who will protect; and raise for us from you one who will help.

(Nisa' 4:75)

Obviously, the oppression of a particular regime is not to be determined by comparing the values and conduct of that regime with Islamic norms and standards, but rather it is to be determined with respect to the free expression of faith. Corruption and mismanagement should not be considered, therefore, the criteria that classify a particular regime as oppressive—deserving, thus, to be fought—because, it may be recalled, believers are commanded to invite others to true faith through friendly means and to effect social and political change using the peaceful methods of education and moral reformation. Only when their peaceful efforts are frustrated and met with violence are they justified to use violence to subdue the aggressive party.

The Prophet did not resort to war against the pagan Arabs until they persecuted the Muslims and violated their lives and properties; nor did he fight the Jews of Medina until they betrayed the Muslims and conspired with their enemies. Similarly, the Prophet declared war against Byzantium and its Arab allies only when they killed the messengers and missionaries who were sent to peacefully teach people Islam and introduce to them the new revelation of God.

CONDUCT OF WAR

3. Proportionality in the Use of Force

The use of force to repel aggression should be in proportion to the harm and damage inflicted by the attackers:

Whoever then acts aggressively against you, inflict injury on him according to the injury he has inflicted on you and be careful (of your duty) to God and know that God is with those who guard (against evil).

(Baqarah 2:194)

4. Only Armed Combatants May Be a Direct Target of Violence

The Qur'an is clear that human life is sacred and cannot be taken except in the case of the individual implicated in murder or violation of human life.

We ordained for the children of Israel that if any one killed a person—unless it be for murder or for spreading mischief in the land—it would be as if he

killed the entire humanity: and if any one saved a life, it would be as if he
saved the life of the whole people.

(Ma'idah 5:32)

Jihad is a central concept in the Qur'an and in Muslim consciousness,
and the effort to equate it with sheer violence and "holy war" is
misguided and dangerous. The term *"jihad"* is as central to Islamic faith
as the word "struggle" to any vibrant and free society. Used in the
broader sense, *jihad* involves struggle to attain moral discipline and to
ensure that injustice and aggression do not go unchallenged.

CHAPTER 20

Shari'ah Principles

Interpreting the Islamic sources (the Qur'an and the prophetic tradition) has become a contentious issue with the rise of popular demands in several Muslim countries to marry the traditional notion of *shari'ah* (Islamic law) with modern social and political institutions. These demands are received with great apprehension by those who erroneously equate *shari'ah* with corporal punishment and the subjugation of women and non-Muslims.

Shari'ah, while often associated with a severe penal code that includes stoning, hand cutting, and corporal punishment, encompasses a broad area of moral concerns. *Shari'ah* involves a set of values that includes emphasis on fair treatment, honesty, charity to the poor and needy, the giving of care and support to neighbors and kin, the honoring of promises and contracts, and obligation to parents, children, relatives, and spouses. *Shari'ah*, further, includes prohibition of extramarital relations, usury, and exploitation. Some *shari'ah* principles have moral bearings, while others have legal consequences as well.

At the heart of the debate over the relevance of *shari'ah* to modern life lies a number of critical questions: what is *shari'ah* and how does it relate to modern society? Is *shari'ah* a legal system concerned with regulating public space? Is *shari'ah* a legal code that can be enforced in society in general? Is it a moral code relevant to the moral choices of Muslims? Or is it the rituals that define the religious practices of Muslims?

MEANING OF *SHARI'AH*

The Qur'an does not use the term *"shari'ah"* in reference to a penal code or a particular set of legal rules but in relation to the guiding principles revealed by God to instruct the actions of the believers:

> We did aforetime grant to the children of Israel the book, the power of command, and prophethood; we gave them, for sustenance, things good and pure; and we favored them above the nations. And we granted them clear signs in affairs (of religion): it was only after knowledge had been granted to them that they fell into schisms, through insolent envy among themselves; verily your Lord will judge between them on the day of judgment as to those matters in which they set up differences. Then we put you on the (right) way of conduct [shari'ah]: so follow that (way), and follow not the desires of those who know not.
>
> (Jathiyah 45:16–18)

The Qur'an further points out that the "way of conduct" expected of the recipients of Islamic revelation differs from the ways required from the followers of earlier revelations. The variation in requirements sets the religious communities apart in certain conduct, but it does not deny the essential truth shared by all divine revelations.

> To you we sent the scripture in truth, confirming the scripture that came before it, and guarding it in safety: so judge between them by what God has revealed, and follow not their vain desires, diverging from the truth that has come to you. To each among you have we prescribed a direction and an open way. If God had so willed, he would have made you a single people, but (his plan is) to test you in what he has given you; so strive as in a race in all virtues. The goal of you all is to God; it is he that will show you the truth of the matters in which you dispute.
>
> (Ma'idah 5:48)

The differences between the Islamic "way" and that of other revealed "ways" are quite pronounced at the level of rituals, while all divine revelations share a set of core values, including respect of human life, property, and compassion towards the less fortunate in society.

Shari'ah is used by the Qur'an to refer to the rules of conduct prescribed by the Divine and embodied in the Islamic revelation. *Shari'ah* rules must therefore be distinguished from the rules derived by Islamic scholars that constitute the subject of *fiqh,* or Islamic jurisprudence. The confusion, though, often comes from the equation of *shari'ah* with *fiqh,* but the difference between the two is remarkable. *Fiqh* represents the outcome of the human endeavor to apply the principles of *shari'ah* in a given social milieu, and it is therefore colored by the cultural experiences and rational limitations of Muslim scholars in any historical period.

SHARI'AH IS NOT A STATE LAW

Historically, actions and relationships are evaluated in accordance with a scale of five moral standards. According to Islamic jurisprudence, an act may be classified as obligatory (*wajib*), recommended (*mandub*), permissible (*mubah*), reprehensible (*makruh*), or prohibited (*haram*). These five categories reflect the varying levels of moral demands placed on human beings by the divine will. Actions that fall in the first and fifth categories are strictly demanded, whereas acts falling in the second and the fourth categories, around the neutral center of the scale, are not as solemnly demanded; and hence their violation, though discouraged, is not condemned. Put differently, while the individual is obligated morally to follow the commands of the first and last categories—that is, the obligatory and the prohibited—he or she is only encouraged to observe the commands of the second and fourth—that is, the recommended and the reprehensible.

It should be emphasized, however, that even the absolute commands of the *shari'ah* have essentially moral—or more accurately, religious—implications, and thus they are not necessarily under state sanction. For instance, the pilgrimage to Makkah once in a lifetime is obligatory (*wajib*) for every Muslim who is physically and financially capable of performing this duty. Yet the state, according to *shari'ah*, may claim no authority to compel the individual to fulfill this personal obligation. This understanding is in full congruence with the scope of political authority recognized by Prophet Muhammad, as was expressed in the document that set the legal obligations of the members of the first political society established by early Muslims, expounded through the Compact of Medina.

The Compact of Medina established a number of important political principles that, put together, formed the political constitution of the first Islamic polity, defined the political rights and duties of the members of the newly established political community—Muslims and non-Muslims alike, and drew up the political structure of the nascent society. The Medina Compact adopted the principle of religious autonomy based on the freedom of belief of all the members of society. It conceded to the Jews the right to act according to the principles and rulings in which they believed: "The Jews of Banu Auf are one community with the believers. The Jews have their religion and the Muslims theirs."[1]

The Compact stressed that justice was the fundamental principle that would define the relationship among the members of the new multireligious society of Medina. "The Jews must bear their expenses and the Muslims their expenses. Each must help the other against anyone who attacks the people of this Compact. They must seek mutual advice and consultation." It prohibited the Muslims from doing injustice to the Jews or retaliating for their Muslim brothers against the followers of the Jewish religion without adhering to the principles of truth and justice. "To the Jew who follows us belongs help and equality. He shall not be wronged nor shall his enemies be aided."[2]

---

[1] Ibn Hisham, *Al-Sirah Al-Nabawiyah* (Dar Al-Kunuz Al-Adabiyah), vol. 2, p. 501–502.
[2] Ibid.

Further, the Compact stipulated that social and political activities in the new system must be subject to a set of universal values and standards that would treat all people equally. Sovereignty in society would not rest with the rulers, or any particular group, but with the law founded on the basis of justice, goodness, and maintaining the equal dignity of all. The Compact emphasized repeatedly and frequently the fundamentality of justice, goodness, and righteousness, and it condemned in different expressions injustice and tyranny, establishing a number of basic rights for all. These rights included (1) the obligation to help the oppressed; (2) outlawing guilt by association, which was commonly practiced by pre-Islamic Arab tribes: "A person is not liable for his ally's misdeeds"; (3) freedom of belief: "The Jews have their religion and the Muslims have theirs;" and (4) freedom of movement from and to Medina: "Whoever will go out is safe, and whoever will stay in Medina is safe except those who wronged (others), or committed sin."[3]

COMMUNITY-SANCTIONED APPLICATION

Shari'ah, it must be stressed, does not consist of the rules derived by jurists at a particular time and place, but rather it consists of the universal principles embodied in the Islamic revelation that form the basis for jurisprudence. *Shari'ah* must not therefore be equated with state law, and it has never been understood as such by Islam's Prophet and leading Muslim jurists.

The problem in relating *shari'ah* to contemporary society results from the erroneous assumption that *shari'ah* is the law to be enforced by the state. Early Muslim scholars recognized the moral and religious autonomy of the social groups that constituted the diverse society in which they lived. They understood very well that political authority is firmly grounded in a social contract that defines the political rights and obligations of both the rulers and the ruled. Al-Mawardi, for instance, argues in his important work *Al-Ahkam Al-Sultaniyyah* (the rules of political authority) that the authority of the ruler (*imam*) is derived from the contractual relationship with the representatives of social groups.[4]

Early scholars were also clear that the social contract extended to other faith groups. Muhammad bin Al-Hasan Al-Shaybani states, for example, in unequivocal terms that when non-Muslims enter into a peace covenant with Muslims, "Muslims should not appropriate any of their [the non-Muslims'] houses and land, nor should they intrude into any of their dwellings. Because they have become party to a covenant of peace, and because on the day of the [peace of] Khaybar, the prophet's spokesman announced that none of the property of the covenanter is permitted to

---

[3]Ibn Hisham, *Al-Sirah Al-Nabawiyah* (Dar Al-Kunuz Al-Adabiyah), vol. 2, p. 501–502.
[4]Al-Mawardi, *Al-Ahkam Al-Sultaniyyah* (Dar Al-Fikr), p. 59.

them [the Muslim]. Also because they [the non-Muslims] have accepted the peace covenant so as they may enjoy their properties and rights on par with Muslims."[5]

Al-Shaybani's emphasis on the equal dignity extended to the People of the Book came in the context of asserting the rights of non-Muslims to follow practices acceptable to their religious communities—even when they conflict with what Muslims consider to be right and proper—such as raising pigs and drinking wine. Al-Shaybani asserted, in effect, that the *fiqh* rules do not apply to followers of other revealed books, and he asserted that it is part of *shari'ah* that non-Muslims enjoy their moral autonomy and apply their morally and religiously sanctioned rules.

Indeed, in Muslim communities, judges did not base their decisions on abstract notions but on moral consensus and established traditions (*'urf*). An examination of the judicial procedures in traditional Muslim society shows that judges did not rely on jurisprudential doctrines expounded by prominent jurists but rather on the community consensus. Put differently, jurisprudential doctrines did not bear directly on the rulings of traditional Muslim judges, but rather they impacted judicial positions through the filter of community consensus. As such, the jurist impact was primarily educational, in that his doctrinal position affected the understanding and commitments of social actors.

SHARI'AH PRINCIPLES OVER FIQH RULES

A major flaw in contemporary popular understanding of *shari'ah* lies in the failure to recognize that the rules of *shari'ah*—even those that are explicitly elaborated in the Qur'an, such as the categories of the persons eligible to receive *zakah* or the penalty specified for criminal conduct—do not mechanically apply but are subject to considerations that take into account principles of higher demand. Ultimately, the application of *shari'ah* rules must recognize the principles of justice and higher good. Paying attention to higher principles of *shari'ah* and its underlying purposes was practiced by the companions of the Prophet, and it was later elaborated into the science of the principles of jurisprudence by Muslim scholars.

Umar bin Al-Khattab, for instance, suspended the application of the punishment of theft during famine years, recognizing that some people did resort to stealing food because they were deprived from resources. He also decided to suspend the Qur'anic directive to make monetary compensation to unsympathetic tribal leaders as a means to procure their supports (*al-mualafati qulubuhum*), on the ground that the emerging community was not anymore in need to procure such support. Muslim jurists

---

[5]Muhammad bin Ahmad Al-Sarakhsi, *Sharh Kitab Al-Siyar Al-Kabir* (Nusrullah Mansour), vol. 4, p. 1530.

must, therefore, subordinate detailed rules of *fiqh* to the establish principles of *shari'ah*. A working woman, for instance, who shares with her
husband her personal earnings, must not be subject to the rules
expounded by early jurists in society. Working women who contribute
to the household must be given fair share of the collective wealth of
the family, and they should not be subjected to the same *fiqh* rules applied
historically to social settings in which women never contributed to the
household and could often find financial support from their extended
family.

The prominent Jurist Ibn Al-Qiyyim got it right when he asserted that
"shari'ah directives must always be rooted in the principle of justice"
(I'lam Al-Muwaqi'in).

PART V

UNIVERSAL PEACE

Community peace is brought about by forging bonds and ties among like-minded individuals who form the community. The community is distinguished by strong bonds and unbroken solidarity among its members, since the ties that bring the members of the community together are the very values and beliefs that form the individual consciousness. Deep faith and commitment to the Divine are at the foundation of community solidarity.

Universal peace is, on the other hand, achieved in a pluralistic society that comprises of competing social groups. This peace rests on the notion of individual rights and the recognition that people are intrinsically free, and that their freedom is vital for human creativity, maturation, and growth. While community peace is a precondition for universal peace, the latter allows individuals and groups to reevaluate their performance and learn from both the strengths and weaknesses of others. As a result, universal peace both reaffirms and enriches inner and community peace.

The struggle for universal peace requires tremendous moral and spiritual strength, as the endeavor to achieve and maintain justice faces its most trying and difficult test. Universal peace is, therefore, not only the culmination of inner and social peace, but it constitutes a crucial precondition for their further development and maturation.

CHAPTER 21

Recognition and Equal Dignity

Equality is not, and has never been, an empirical experience. The empirical and practical experiences of humans suggest that people are markedly different in their intellectual, emotional, physical, financial, and moral capacities. The people we meet every day occupy a wide range of inequality in every aspect of life, to the extent that we can locate them anywhere on a continuum between a host of extremes. People may be described as either extraordinarily intelligent or extremely dumb, remarkably courageous or exceedingly cowardly, greatly generous or abhorrently mean, admirably diligent and accomplished or sadly lazy and mediocre, quite wealthy or very poor, and so on.

If people are quite different in capacity and impact, in what sense can we talk about human equality?

Well, the only way we can do that is by invoking the concept of dignity, insisting that all people are equal in dignity and that they all share the same human essence. Our conception of human equality is, therefore, based on theoretical assertions rather than any empirical experience. Put more accurately, our assertion that people share equal dignity is literally borne out of faith.

Many people today take the notion of human equality for granted, but this belief has not always been rampant for the bulk of human history. In most pre-Islamic societies, the notion of equal dignity of all people was rejected. The Romans, for instance, considered themselves superior to non-Romans. This asserted inequality was emphasized by the Roman law that governed Pax Romana that was enforced by the Roman empire over countless nations and tribes. Even within the privileged ethnic Romans, inequality of individuals of Roman background was assumed and accepted, and during the last few centuries of the empire, emperors were considered to enjoy divine qualities and status.

Similarly, the Jewish tribes who lived in central Arabia near Medina espoused a sense of superiority over the Bedouin Arabs who lived nearby. The Arab tribes were illiterate and subscribed to pagan religious traditions that recognized no universal values and commitments. In dealing with the pagan Arabs, the cultured Hebrew tribes developed a supremacist attitude and insisted that they were not required to respect the rights of their pagan neighbors. "They say we are under no obligation to keep faith with the illiterates" (Al 'Imran 3:75), the Qur'an points out.

Pre-Islamic Arabs, likewise, considered themselves to be superior to other nations, as they showed great pride in their autonomy and freedom, something that no other community in the surrounding regions could claim or match. They divided the world into two categories: Arab and Ajam. The word the pre-Islamic Arabs used to refer to other people, "*ajam*" or "*A'ajim*," is the same word they used to refer to animals. The Qur'an rejects the notion of the supremacy of any tribal or ethnic group, and it asserts the intrinsic dignity and equality of all people:

> O humans! We created you from a single (pair) of a male and a female, and made you into nations and tribes, that you may know each other (not that you may despise each other). Verily the most honored of you in the sight of God is (he who is) the most righteous of you. And God has full knowledge and is well-acquainted (with all things).
>
> (Hujurat 49:13)

> We gave dignity for the sons of Adam; provided them with transport on land and sea; given them for sustenance things good and pure; and conferred on them special favors, above a great part of our creation.
>
> (Isra' 17:70)

The dignity the Qur'an refers to is a privilege given to all human beings, not only those who show faith and follow divine revelation. This dignity is associated with the human condition as well as human qualities and mission, which set humans apart from many other creatures. Humans are honored by their intellectual capacity, free will, and the ability to transform their ideas and thoughts to objects and actions. We will see in the next chapter that human dignity is directly linked with the individual freedom and moral autonomy that together entitle people to pursue self-identified goals and purposes. We will consider in the current chapter, however, the question of the equal dignity of all people.

PAROCHIALISM AND EXCLUSIVISM

All religious communities have shown propensity to display contempt to followers of other religious traditions. The contemptuous attitude often represents a self-defensive mechanism borne out of the need to highlight the lines of demarcation between religious traditions, rather than any revealed commandments. This attitude can be found among all religious communities, including Judaism, Christianity, and Islam. The Qur'an was critical of the exclusivist and contemptuous attitudes of certain followers of early revelations, particularly the followers of Judaism and Christianity, and it discussed at length their exclusivist and self-righteous claims.

The Qur'an insists that a critical mass of the children of Israel, the descendents of Prophet Ya'qub (Jacob), failed to keep the legacy he was keen to pass to them, because they embraced a distorted conception of religion and religiosity. They embraced an egotistic conception of religion, in which religion was used as an instrument to elevate the self and to disdain the other. Religion was taken as an exclusive identity used to celebrate one's self-importance and self-glory, rather than a mission to advance the cause of God and celebrate his glory.

The failure of Banu Israel to heed the divine directives and embrace the divine will, and their insistence on using religion for the purpose of confessing their self-importance, has been documented in the Qur'an so that Muslims can learn from past failures and mistakes of a community of faith:

> And they say: None shall enter paradise unless he be a Jew or a Christian. Those are their (vain) desires. Say: Produce your proof if you are truthful.
>
> (Baqarah 2:111)

> Both the Jews and the Christians say: We are the children of God, and his beloved ones. Say: Why then does he punish you for you sins? Nay you are but humans of the humans he created.
>
> (Ma'idah 5:18)

Banu Israel's misconception of religion and their misunderstanding of the meaning of a life of faith led them to commit injustices against their neighbors and other communities. Again the Qur'an documents their transgression in the name of religion:

> They say we are under no obligation to keep faith with the illiterates (Arab pagans). But they tell a lie against God and (well) they know it.
>
> (Al 'Imran 3:75)

Banu Israel transformed God's revelation into a form of nationalism, a religious nationalism, whereby they became bound not by moral commitments and faith, but by group interests.

Today, there are Muslims who repeat the same mistakes committed by early religious communities, mistakes that the Qur'an rejects and repudiates, by advancing the same claims the Qur'an criticizes and rejects. The fact that the Qur'an did not criticize Muslims by name for claiming exclusive access to salvation and divine mercy does not mean that Muslims have license to repeat the same mistakes. If it was wrong for pre-Islamic Jewish and Christian communities to claim monopoly over salvation, it is still wrong for Muslims to do it today.

PROMOTING GOOD AND DEFENDING RIGHTS

One important challenge that confronts individuals who live in a multireligious society is how to display strong commitment to the rule of law when the people subscribe to different value systems. The challenge, while more pronounced across religions, could also be experienced within the same religious community. How could people who belong to diverse religious communities support a system of law when they espouse different interpretations and understandings of the notions of right and wrong? Which of the competing value systems should be elevated to the level of a legal order publicly enforced?

The Qur'an directs the believers to advance established rights and to reform social conditions so as to accord with sublime moral principles. Reforming social practices and ensuring that good triumphs over evil, and right over wrong, are paramount obligations of all people of faith. All prophets were sent with the explicit mission of reforming their societies and overcoming evil and wrongdoing.

Indeed, the early Muslim community's greatest achievement was in establishing a society committed to a system of checks and balances, promoting moral practices, and rejecting corruption:

> You were the best of people evolved for mankind, enjoining what is right, forbidding what is wrong, and believing in God.
>
> (Al 'Imran 3:110)

The above verse is sometimes misinterpreted as to confer a position of superiority on the Muslim community. This distorted understanding is the result of gross misreading of the verse, as it is intended to describe the pioneering Muslim community that struggled despite great odds, and with remarkable devotion, to translate Islamic teachings into a living community. The only way that this verse can be used in reference to any contemporary community is by insisting that this community resembles, in its devotion to God and its commitment to the principle of enjoining the right and forbidding the wrong, the early Muslim community. Still, the judgment of whether the above stipulated condition is met will have to be left to the divine judgment, as it could not be ascertained with confidence by living humans, certainly not by those who are intended by the verse. To ensure that human societies steer away from corruption and maintain high moral standards, the Qur'an directs Muslims to ensure that a group of them is continuously charged with the task of enjoining what is right and forbidding evil.

Let there arise out of you a band of people inviting to all that is good, enjoining what is right, and forbidding what is wrong: they are the ones to attain felicity.

(Al 'Imran 3:105)

The Qur'an, however, does not only point out the mission but also underscores the importance of the method and the strategy for achieving it. The Qur'an emphasizes the importance of good manners and the need to respect community norms and choices.

Enjoining the right is not, it must be stressed, a license to impose the values and beliefs of a religious, sectarian, or confessional community on the rest of society. Far from it. The Qur'an makes it abundantly clear that what is to be enjoined is what is "agreeable" or commonly shared (*ma'ruf*). If it is not widely acceptable it cannot be enjoined but rather has to be promoted; hence the call for promoting the good by manner of invitation (*yad'una ila al-khair*). The Qur'an directs the believers to invite to good practices, to only enjoin those practices that are considered agreeable by society, and to oppose practices that are deemed evil and intolerable by society.

Invite (all) to the way of your Lord with wisdom and beautiful preaching; and argue with them in ways that are best and most gracious: for your Lord knows best who have strayed from his path and who receive guidance.

(Nahl 16: 125)

It is with the mercy of God that you do deal gently with them. Were you severe or harsh-hearted, they would have broken away from you.

(Al 'Imran 3:159)

Further, the Qur'an is consistent in its use of the terms "invite" or "call" and the terms "enjoin" or "command." Muslims are told to invite to the good and to command commonly accepted norms and values. "Hold to forgiveness, command what is customary (*'urf*), but turn away from the ignorant" (A'raf 7:199).

The distinction between the "good" and the "agreeable" is not trivial but essential for avoiding any distortion in the mission and purpose of Islam. It is essential to ensure that Islam and its mission is seen and felt as a mercy to mankind, commanding the respect of people, that it does not deteriorate into a repressive force. Creating moral consensus in society comes first. And when that is done, individuals can command what is already recognized as good. It is with this understanding that one can make sense of the prophetic traditions that ask the believer to take action to stop corruption. Imam Bukhari reported the following *hadith*: "Whoever witnesses wrongdoing, let him change it with his hand, if he cannot, let him change it by his tongue, and if he still cannot, let him reject it by his heart, and this is the weakest of faith." Faith in the service of humanity and devotion to God must never lead a person to feel superior or act with arrogance but must always prompt people to serve other human beings, particularly the weak and less fortunate. This understanding lies at the heart of the Qur'anic message, as it is the hallmark of the prophetic tradition. The Qur'an stresses time and again that a life of faith is a life spent to benefit humanity and improve human conditions and to ensure that justice, mutual help, and compassion prevail in society.

The mission of the Prophet, and hence the Islamic mission, is defined in the Qur'an as one of mercy to humanity:

> We have sent you not but as a mercy to all beings.
>
> (Anbiya' 21:17)

The object of mercy and the beneficiaries of the Islamic revelation are not exclusively the followers of Islam, but humanity at large:

> Alif Lam Raa, a book which we have revealed unto you, in order that you may lead the people out of the depth of darkness into light—by the leave of their Lord—to the way of the Exalted in power, the Worthy of all praise.
>
> (Ibrahim 14:1)

The Prophet exemplified the life of faith in which the faithful is devoted to the betterment of all human beings, as he was devoted to the mission delineated by the Qur'an as a "mercy to all beings." There are many instances in the life of the Prophet to illustrate his mission of mercy. Suffice it here to point to two telling moments when he would have been justified in withholding generosity and mercy. The first moment is when Archangel Gabriel came to him after he was driven out of the city of Ta'if and humiliated by its inhabitants, who encouraged their youth to chastise him out of the town. Gabriel told him: "Command me O Muhammad to bring these two mountains over their city." Even though this was a moment of anguish and pain in which people are usually inclined to vent their anger on their enemies, the Prophet's response was: "I hope that one day there will rise among their progeny people who will submit to the will of God and will not associate other deity with him" (Ibn Hisham).

Another illustrative moment showing clearly that Prophet Muhammad was committed to the principle of equal dignity of all people, rather than to religiosity as a self-glorifying identity, was the Conquest of Makkah. The Prophet entered the city triumphant after he, and his companions, were driven out from the city and were oppressed, then militarily attacked, for many years by its inhabitants. In the custom of the pagan culture of Arabia the Prophet was expected to ransack the city, kill its male inhabitants, and enslave the females and children. Instead, he gathered its people and told them: "Go to your daily business, you shall remain free people" (Ibn Hisham).

It is important to emphasize here that this was not a prophetic moment with no equivalence in the life of the Muslim community. The mission of mercy, liberation, and concern for the dignity of humanity inspired over the centuries different generations of Muslims. A similar moment, one that was recorded by both Muslim and non-Muslim historians, appears during the Muslims' triumph over the crusaders, under the leadership of Salahuddin (Saladin). When the victorious Muslim army entered Jerusalem, after 100 years of brutal occupation that began with a massacre that claimed the life of most of its inhabitants, Muslims and Christians alike, Salahuddin and his army were not vindictive and sought no revenge. Instead, they treated their enemies with humanity, spared their lives, and gave them the choice to go back to Europe from where they had come or stay in peace in the city.

Evidently, the Qur'an wants its followers to engage people of diverse religious and confessional backgrounds, as it urges them to show care and respect toward diverse humanity. The Qur'an advances an unmistakably humanistic outlook, and it places a high premium on human life and dignity—so much so that it considers benefiting people in general (*alnas*) the criteria by which to distinguish between vain life and actions and those that have a lasting impact. As the Qur'an puts it:

> Thus does God (by parables) show forth truth and falsehood (vanity). For the scum disappears like froth cast out; while that which is for the good of mankind remains on earth.
>
> (Ra'd 13:17)

CHAPTER 22

Responsible Freedom

There is no quality of human life that is more precious after intelligence than freedom. Countless people throughout human history chose death over life when life could only be had under conditions of servitude. No cause has ever justified fighting and war more than freedom. The cry "Give me liberty or give me death," popularized by Patrick Henry, is a modern-time rendering of a principle as old as human society.

The Qur'an was revealed in a society that cherished freedom. For the pre-Islamic Arabs, freedom was the only thing that made life worth living in the harsh and resource-scarce region of Arabia, a vast desert land with a limited number of oases. The Qur'an came to reassert human freedom but also to redefine it in ways that would make it compatible with justice and social harmony. The freedom the Qur'an anticipates is a responsible freedom, whereby the free choices taken by the individual are guided by the obligations a person has towards God and other human beings.

TAKING RESPONSIBILITY FOR CHOICES AND ACTIONS

Human beings are naturally inclined to assert their own wills, and they are frustrated and angered if their freedom to do that is taken away or severely curtailed. While freedom is cherished by humans, not all people exercise their freedom responsibly. Failure to exercise responsible freedom results from one of two extreme positions—it results from either denying that human actions are the consequences of free choices or from insisting that people have absolute freedom to change things at will. We will categorize the first position under "determinism," and the other under "anarchism." As will be argued below, both positions are rejected and refuted by the Qur'an. Determinism holds that all events and happenings are completely determined by the divine will and hence are irresponsive to the human will. This position has often been taken as a ground for denying human accountability.

> Those who give partners (to God) will say: If God had wished, we should not have given partners to him, nor would our fathers: nor should we have had any taboos. So did their ancestors argue falsely, until they tasted of our wrath. Say: Have you any (certain) knowledge? If so, produce it before us. You follow nothing but conjecture: you do nothing but lie.
>
> (An'am 6:148)

On the other extreme stand those who believe that the world is spontaneously and immediately responsive to the human will. This position is often adopted by individuals and groups who feel that their faith in God entitles them to a special status and more-privileged position and that they have a God-given license to impose their will on the world. This has often led, historically, to ethnic, racial, or religious supremacist positions and movements. This conception is enforced by the fact that the Qur'an entrusts the believers with the mission of resisting evil and corruption and promoting good and justice, and that the Qur'an promises to vindicate those who accept faith. But this is based on a partial reading and partial understanding of the revealed message of the Qur'an. A more thorough reading shows that the truth lies in a middle ground between the two extremes.

The Qur'an strikes a balanced position between those of "the human will does not matter" and "only the human will matters." A human being has a great scope of freedom to act both in the natural and social orders. But his or her freedom is constrained by various conditions that limit the extent to which both the individual will and the collective will can be realized. It was long before the intellectual and technological capacities of humans were developed so as to allow them to break out of the natural constraints of Planet Earth that the Qur'an encouraged humans to contemplate such a possibility:

> O you of the communities of *jinns* and human beings! If you could pass beyond the outskirts of the heavens and the earth; do so! Though not without authority shall you be able to pass.
>
> (Rahman 55:33)

The Qur'an calls on people to exercise their freedom by bringing their intellectual, emotional, moral, and spiritual qualities to bear on the world that has been bequeathed to them. Humans must be responsive to their natural and social environments, and they must respond in positive ways that go beyond self-satisfaction and self-gratification. A person whose passions can only respond to his personal needs, and who is only concerned with his own personal life, has long abandoned the true purpose of life.

Leave them alone, to eat and enjoy themselves, let false hopes amuse them: soon will knowledge (undeceive them).

(Hijr 15:3)

A truly free person is a passionate human being, whose passions are aligned with the divine purpose of life and whose actions are, therefore, guided by the principles of revelation. To be free is to be active, not passive, to get involved in society and not to withdraw from it. To be free is to be responsible, and hence to be responsive to events and happenings; to express oneself and to use one's abilities to advance the overall purpose of life; to spend out of one's wealth, and to assert the principles of truth and goodness; and to stand up to injustice and wrongdoing, and to take stance in society.

Believe in God and his messenger, and spend (in charity) out of the (substance) whereof he has made you heirs.

(Hadid 57:7)

True freedom goes hand in hand with responsibility and the wise use of the resources and powers that humans possess and enjoy.

THE INTRINSIC DIGNITY OF HUMAN LIFE

The Qur'an describes the human person as a unique being among the creatures of God, endowed with rational capacity to understand the natural order and to distinguish right from wrong. Human beings, the Qur'an stresses, have been elevated over the entire creation by their moral and intellectual capacities, as well as by their ability to translate ideas and values into physical and social forms. Life is presented as a trial in which humans have the opportunity to make choices and are individually responsible for the choices they make. Central to the notion of dignity is the notion of moral autonomy, that is, the freedom to make rational choices and to accept the outcome of the rational choices one makes. At the heart of the notion of dignity, though, is not social license to do whatever one wishes, but a moral character that acts out of deep convictions— including the conviction that one ought to respect the moral choices of others, as well as the expectation that others should reciprocate and respect one's choices. That is, dignity lies in the profound sense of moral autonomy which enables the person to behave in accordance with his or her moral commitments and convictions, regardless of whether others agree with him or her or approve of his or her choices.

It is for this very reason that the behavior of those who are willing to give up their moral autonomy, in exchange for personal gratification, brings to mind the image of a shameless act deprived of dignity—while those who are ready to withstand adversities, even ridicule, rather than betray their moral commitments or submit to the arbitrary will of others make us appreciate human dignity. Although the individual sense of dignity cannot be taken away, but can only be strengthened, by the use of arbitrary force to restrict moral autonomy, belief in human equality and the transcendental nature of moral responsibility requires that the moral autonomy of the individual be protected, by a system of rights, from violation by others, particularly by a superior power, such as the state, or an organized social group. A person who refuses to compromise deeply held principles in exchange for a generous monetary reward or in the face of a serious threat to one's safety, exemplifies human dignity at its best.

Yet moral autonomy associated with human dignity is not limited to the individual, but involves the moral autonomy of the group to which one belongs as well. Because the concretization of the moral choices one makes requires the cooperation of all individuals who share the same moral vision, the autonomy of individuals—and hence their dignity—hinges on the autonomy of the group to which they belong. It is here where the meanings of individuality in the Occidental and Muslim historical experiences diverge. In the Occidental tradition, the individual is seen as a member of a homogeneous community, and the freedom of the individual means that he has the right to enact his moral choices, as long as they do not violate the freedom of others. However, in traditional Islamic thought and experience, society was not seen as homogenous but rather as consisting of a plurality of moral communities, each of which has the freedom to actualize its own moral vision.

Emphasizing the moral autonomy of groups is exceedingly important in a postmodern society that combines global orientation with moral and cultural fragmentation. The homogenous culture in which Western individualism was developed has already become something of the past. Cultural fragmentation and the coexistence of a multitude of moral communities is today the reality of societies that once enjoyed remarkable cultural homogeneity, such as the French and the German. Protecting human dignity in a heterogeneous society requires a markedly new approach, whereby the moral autonomy of the individual is linked to that of the moral community to which he or she belongs. Recognizing the moral autonomy of groups in traditional Muslim society meant that religious minorities enjoyed the freedom not only to profess their own religious values, but also to live in accordance with the dictates of these values, and to be able to apply a system of law that was compatible with those values.

RELIGIOUS FREEDOM

Freedom of religion is enshrined in the Qur'an. There is ample evidence in the Qur'an that individuals should be able to accept or reject a particular faith on the basis of personal conviction, and that no amount of external pressure or compulsion should be permitted. The freedom to choose one's faith and subscribe to a system of morality and law that is compatible with it is equally true for Muslims and non-Muslims.

> No compulsion in religion: truth stands out clear from error.
>
> (Baqarah 2:256)

> If it had been the Lord's will, they would have believed—all who are on earth! Will you then compel mankind, against their will, to believe!
>
> (Yunus 10:99)

> Say, the truth is from your Lord: Let him who will, believe, and let him who will, reject (it) for the wrongdoers we have prepared a fire whose smoke and flame will surround them.
>
> (Kahf 18:29)

By emphasizing people's right to freely follow their convictions, the Qur'an reiterates a long-standing position that it traces back to one of the earliest known Prophets, Noah:

> He [Noah] said: O my people! See if I have a clear sign from my Lord, and that he has sent mercy unto me, but that the mercy has been obscured from your sight? Shall we compel you to accept it when you are averse to it?
>
> (Hud 11:28)

The message of freedom of belief and conviction, and the call to religious tolerance, is reiterated time and time again through various prophets, as it is quite apparent in the message of Prophet Shuaib to his people:

> And if there is a party among you that believes in the message with which I have been sent, and a party which does not believe, hold yourselves in patience until God does decide between us: for he is the best to decide.
>
> (A'raf 7:87)

When Shuaib's people threatened him with expulsion, he protested strongly, citing his freedom to choose his faith:

> The leaders, the arrogant party among his people, said: O Shuaib! We shall certainly drive you out of our city, and those who believe with you, or else you shall have to return to our ways and religion. He said: What? Even though we do not wish to do so.
>
> (A'raf 7:88)

Not only does the Qur'an recognize the individual's right to freedom of conviction, but it also recognizes his/her moral freedom to act on the basis of that conviction.

> Say: O my people! Do whatever you may: I will do (my part). But soon will you know on whom an anguish of ignoring shall be visited, and on whom descends an anguish that will abide.
>
> (Zumar 39:39–40)

Say: Everyone acts according to his own disposition: but your Lord knows
best who it is that is best guided on the way.

(Isra' 17:84)

The principle that the larger community has no right to interfere in
one's choices of faith and conviction can be seen, further, in the fact that
the Qur'an emphasizes that the individual is accountable for the moral
choices he or she makes in this life to the creator alone:

O you who believe! Guard your own souls: if you follow (right) guidance, no
hurt can come to you from those who stray. The goal of you all is God: it is he
that will show you the truth of all that you do.

(Ma'idah 5:105)

So if they dispute with you, say: I have submitted my whole self to God and
so have those who follow me. And say to the People of the Book and to those
who are unlearned: Do you (also) submit yourselves? If they do, they are in
right guidance. But if they turn back, your duty is to convey the message;
and in God's sight are (all) his servants.

(Al 'Imran 3:20)

Indeed, one cannot find in the Qur'an any support for the apostasy
(*ridda*) penalty. The Qur'an makes two references to *ridda*:

Nor will they cease fighting you until they turn you back from your faith if
they can. And if any of you turn back (commits *ridda*) from their faith and
die in that state of unbelief, their works will bear no fruit in this life; and in
the hereafter they will be companions of the fire and will abide therein.

(Baqarah 2:217)

O you who believe! If any from among you turn back (commits *ridda*) from
his/her faith, soon will God produce a people whom he will love as they will
love him—humble with the believers mighty against the disbelievers, thriv-
ing in the way of God, and never afraid of the reproaches of detractors. That
is the grace of God, he bestows on whom he please; and God encompasses all
and he knows all things.

(Ma'idah 5:54)

In both cases the Qur'an does not specify any physical punishment
here and now, let alone a death penalty. The Qur'an rather warns of disgrace and ill fate to those who renounce their faith. To the contrary, the
Qur'an provides direct evidence that *ridda* is not punishable by death:

Those who believe then disbelieve, then believe again, then disbelieve and
then increase in their disbelief—God will never forgive them nor guide them
to the path.

(Nisa' 4:137)

Obviously, a death penalty would not permit repeated conversion from
and to Islam. Freedom of choice and action, cherished immensely by early
Muslims, was stressed strongly in the Qur'an. Umar bin Al-Khattab,

the second Muslim caliph, protested with indignation the abusive behavior of the son of the governor of Egypt during his rule towards an Egyptian native: "Whence did you enslave people when their mothers brought them to live as free human beings," Umar reminded his governor.

The Qur'an, however, expects individual freedom to be used wisely and responsibly. To be free after all is to be accountable for one's choices and actions. Indeed this is the only way for humans to be held accountable. It is common sense that a person who is compelled to act against his will cannot be held accountable for his act. Freedom is, undoubtedly, a precondition for morality, and individuals who are compelled by force to do what is right and avoid evil and wrong cannot claim any moral standing, and they would often indulge in immoral and irresponsible actions as soon as they were able to escape supervision and act on their own.

CHAPTER 23

Justice Is Paramount

There is no value that is given more prominence in the Qur'an than the value of justice. Justice occupies central position in the scheme of all things: divine spirit, the creation of the universe, the composition of the human being, the purpose of revelation, the evolution of human history, and social interaction.

Justice in the Qur'an does not stop at formal and procedural notions but deals with the substantive issues of recognition of rights, distribution of wealth, exploitation of labor, and domination of people. The Qur'an stresses, time and again, that these are not minor issues but relate to a central value of Islam, the value of justice in general and social justice in particular. Justice is so important a value in Islam that the Qur'an makes it a defining element of the individual, the community, and the universe.

DIMENSIONS OF JUSTICE

Justice, though central to life and existence, is an elusive concept, difficult to pin down. The difficulty of defining justice stems from the fact that it is a composite value that anticipates and combines many other values. Justice presupposes a commitment to equality and the ability to take subtle differences into account when dispensing judgment. Justice also requires a sense of responsibility and duty, and it presupposes discipline, respect for diversity, and compassion and care. Justice has several salient meanings in the Qur'an. It is a principle of creation, the purpose of divine revelation, and it stands above social solidarity and political enmity.

Principle of Creation – The Qur'an asserts that justice is a divine quality and a principle of creation. God is not only just; he is justice and his will is the measure of justice. The universe is harmonious and the natural order is fulfilling because it is founded on just measures, and humans are capable of justice because the human spirit emanates from the divine spirit.

Verily, all things have been created in proportion and measure. And our command is but a single (act), like the twinkling of an eye.

(Qamar 54:49–50)

And the heaven he raised high and he set up the balance. So establish weight with justice and fall not short in the balance.

(Rahman 55:7–9)

Purpose of Revelation – Justice is not simply one of the values emphasized in the Qur'an, but it is the value under which others are subsumed. Indeed, justice is the very reason divine revelation came to humanity in the first place:

We sent our messengers with clear signs, and sent down with them the book and the balance that men may stand forth in justice, and we sent down iron, in which is (material for) mighty war, as well as many benefits for mankind, that God may test who it is that will help unseen him and his messenger.

(Hahih 57:25)

Justice above Religious and Social Solidarity – Solidarity with people close to us and with those who share with us similar religious outlook, ethnic heritage, cultural traditions, tribal bonds, or family ties, is a natural instinct and universal inclination. People often find it difficult to take stand against a friend or close relative to protect the rights and interests of a complete stranger. But this exactly what the Qur'an commands. The demands of justice and equity are over and above any other human bond, including the strongest of all, the bond between parents and children.

O you who believe! Stand out firmly for justice, as witnesses to God, even as against yourselves, or your parents, or your kin, and whether it be (against) rich or poor: for God can best protect both. Follow not the lusts (of your hearts), lest you swerve, and if you distort (justice) or decline to do justice, verily God is well acquainted with all that you do.

(Nisa' 4:135)

Justice above Enmity – Not only does ensuring equity require that one support the rights of the wronged party against the excesses of close family members and associates, but it also requires that one maintains fairness towards those who are open enemies.

O you who believe! Stand out firmly for God, as witnesses to fair dealing, and let not the hatred of others to you make you swerve to wrong and depart from justice. Be just: that is next to piety: and fear God, for God is well acquainted with all that you do.

(Ma'idah 5:8)

Justice as Fairness and Maintenance of Covenants – Justice is expected in relation to all people regardless of their social rank and economic status.

Justice requires that one is fair when conducting business transactions, when entering into contractual relationships, and when assuming positions of leadership and authority.

> So establish weight with justice and fall not short in the balance.
>
> (Rahman 55:9)

> God commands you to render back your trusts to those to whom they are due; and when you judge between people, that you judge with justice.
>
> (Nisa' 4:58)

SOCIAL JUSTICE

Justice in the Qur'an does not end with respecting the rights and dignity of others but also involves ensuring just distribution of collective resources. The Qur'anic approach to just distribution of resources focuses on the principles of caring and sharing. The faithful is by definition a person who cares about the plight of others and is willing to share with those in need.

> Have you seen the one who denies the judgment (to come)? Then such as the (man) who repulses the orphan (with harshness), and encourages not the feeding of the indigent. So woe to the worshippers who are neglectful of their prayers, those who (want but) to be seen (of men), but refuse (to supply) (even) neighborly needs.
>
> (Ma'un 107:1–7)

Sharing one's wealth with those who are deprived is an individual responsibility. After all, people must not lose sight of the fact that they are moral agents and that they must always discharge their responsibility in accordance with the duties and obligations of their moral agency.

> Believe in God and his messenger, and spend (in charity) out of the (substance) whereof he has made you heirs. For those of you who believe and spend (in charity) is a great reward.
>
> (Hadid 57:7)

Further, the Qur'an asserts that God requires that wealth is not concentrated in the hands of the more fortunate members of society and that resources must be circulated in ways that can reach the less fortunate members of society.

> What God has bestowed on his messenger (and taken away) from the people of the townships, belongs to God, to his messenger and to kindred and orphans, the needy and the wayfarer; in order that it may not (merely) make a circuit between the wealthy among you. So take what the messenger assigns to you, and deny yourselves that which he withholds from you. And fear God; for God is strict in punishment.
>
> (Hashr 59:7)

JUSTICE AS AN INDIVIDUAL QUALITY

The Qur'an does not regard justice as a reality or force external to the spirit. Justice is not merely a legal concept to be encountered in the court system but a human quality and individual attitude. A just society does not lie in the prescribed laws that regulate social behavior but in the attitudes and moral commitments of its members.

> God put forth a parable of two men: the first is dumb of no power of any sort, and he is completely reliant on his master, wherever his master directs him he brings no good; is he equal with the one who command justice and he is on the right path?
>
> (Nahl 16:76)

In the above verse, the Qur'an gives us an insight into justice as an individual attitude and practice by contrasting the just with the feeble. The feeble (*alkal*) is presented in the above parable as a dumb person who chooses silence when he needs to speak. He is dumb by choice and not because of a physical handicap. He is never able to complete a task; even when he is directed, he fails to effect good.

The just (*al'adl*) is, on the other hand, a person who commands justice, even when he has no commanding position—because when a person demands justic,e he or she immediately assumes a commanding stance. The just person has vision and direction, and he has the discipline to live and act accordingly. He is a free human being, self-reliant, self-initiating, and self-disciplined. The feeble lacks self-initiative and even lacks the discipline to execute instructions and follow directions through—while the just is self-initiating and has a clear vision; his vision is so clear that he does not wait for instructions to take the initiative, because he is a responsible person who sticks to his vision and follows through.

The rhetorical question that the Qur'an raises is straightforward: are the just and feeble equal in their impact on life? The answer is self-evident and intuitive, in need of no further deliberation.

Justice is rooted, the Qur'an tells us, in the individual, and a just society can be realized only when just individuals constitute a critical mass in it. A just society is made of people who are free human beings, who view other human beings as having equal dignity. It is made of people who take initiative and are committed to the principles of right and goodness. It is made of people capable of supporting visionary leaders, who are certain as to what they want to do with their lives. It is a society of principled individuals who have the courage to live their principles and to speak out against injustice and wrongdoing, rather than remaining silent.

CHAPTER 24

Faith in Interfaith

The story of faith is told repeatedly in the Qur'an. It is a moving story of commitment to God and the truth he revealed to humanity, and of the constant struggle to live by the values of devotion, compassion, consideration, and justice. It is the story of a long line of prophets and their followers who put mercy, charity, honesty, and sincerity over and above their short-term personal interests and benefits. All revealed books and all messengers sent by God to guide humanity assert that true and honest living is the assured way for spiritual and social harmony and for protecting the long-term self-interests of every human being.

The Qur'an further asserts that humans are fallible and can never be free of error in understanding and judgment. Human knowledge is imperfect and subject to bias and error. Knowledge of intentions and inner thoughts is beyond human capacity; so is the knowledge of the final destiny of individuals. People of faith must show humility and put their trust in divine wisdom and the absolute justice of God, and they must focus on doing what is right and just, instead of sitting in judgment on the eternal salvation of others. The Qur'an is clear that only God knows who is true and sincere in worship and service and who has gone astray:

> Your Lord knows best who strays from his way: he knows best who they are that receive his guidance.
>
> (An'am 6:117)

> And we granted them clear signs in matters (of religion): it was only after knowledge had been granted to them that they fell into schisms, through insolent envy among themselves. Verily your lord will judge between them on the day of judgment as to those matters in which they set up differences.
>
> (Jathiyah 45:17)

The duty of the faithful is, therefore, not to judge others and look down on those who have different understanding and faith; rather, it is to respect their choices and each one try his or her best to live an upright life and manifest the values of his and her faith through good work and good deeds.

> To you we sent the scripture in truth, confirming the scripture that came before it, and guarding it in safety: so judge between them by what God has revealed, and follow not their vain desires, diverging from the truth that has come to you. To each among you have we prescribed a law and an open way. If God had so willed, he would have made you a single people, but (his plan is) to test you in what he has given you; so strive as in a race in all virtues. The goal of you all is to God; it is he that will show you the truth of the matters in which you dispute.
>
> (Ma'idah 5:48)

The Qur'an came to confirm the truth revealed in early scriptures, and the People of the Book, the followers of the revealed scriptures, have a special place in the Qur'an, particularly those who carry the Abrahamic legacy. Significant portions of the Qur'an focus on the story of the biblical prophets and their followers, the Jews and Christians. It presents their stories as the story of the journey of faith, reminding the followers of the last revelation of the ups and downs in the struggle of the early communities of faith. Some commentators have stressed the downside of that story by focusing on the Qur'anic critique of early communities of faith. The Qur'an has pointed out several excesses and mistakes committed by the followers of the biblical prophets, and it warned the followers of Prophet Muhammad against committing similar excesses.

Yet the Qur'an is also full of stories of great struggles and shining examples found in the followers of early prophets, whose commitment and devotion were crucial for establishing the monotheistic traditions and translating divine guidance into social practices—for example, there is the strong faith of Saul (Talout) and those who stood firmly with him (Baqarah 2:249); the devotion of the people of the Trench, who remained true to their faith in the face of horrifying aggression committed by ruthless enemies (Buruj 85:1–11); and the unwavering commitment of the followers of Christ to the ethical code and compassionate spirit he brought to humanity (Saff 61:14). Prophet Muhammad repeatedly emphasized that his mission was to affirm early revelation and complete divine revelation. He directed early Muslims to seek refuge in Abyssinia, pointing out that the country was ruled by a just Christian king. This was the beginning of an excellent relationship and strong alliance between Muslims and Christians of Abyssinia that lasted for 1000 years.

DIALOGUE

The first Muslim emigrants who escaped the persecution of Quraysh were led by Ja'far bin Abu Talib; they included Uthman bin Affan, Ruqayyah bint Muhammad, Zubayr bin Alawwan, Abdullah bin

Masood, and Abdul Rahman bin Awf. Soon Quraysh became aware of the
migration of Muslims and sent Amr bin Al-'As and Umarah bin Walid to
the court of Najashi (Negus), the king of Abyssinia, and asked him to hand
over the Muslims so that they could be taken back to Makkah. When they
reached his court, Amr bin Al-'As said, "O King of Abyssinia, the people
under your protection have rejected the religion of their ancestors and
have not accepted your religion, and they follow an obscure religion no
one knows about it. We ask you to hand them over to us, so that we could
take them back to their people who know better how to deal with them."

The king summoned the Muslims to his court and said, "What religion
that led you to leave the religion of your people and stay away of my religion or any other religion embraced by the known nations?" Ja'far bin
Abu Talib stepped forward and said: "O king of Abyssinia! We were a
people of ignorance, who worshipped idols, eat un-slaughtered animals,
committed sin, broke family ties, disregarded neighbors, and the strong
among us abused the weak. Then God sent to us a messenger from among
us, whose lineage, honesty, trustworthiness, and integrity were well
known to us. He called us unto God, that we should testify to his oneness
and worship him and renounce what we and our fathers had worshipped
in the way of stones and idols; and he commanded us to speak truly, to
fulfill our promises, to respect the ties of kinship and the rights of our
neighbors, and to refrain from crimes and from bloodshed. . . .Our people
turned against us, and have persecuted us to make us forsake our religion
and revert from the worship of God to the worship of idols." Najashi was
satisfied with Ja'far's response and sent him and his Muslim companions
back, reassured of his continued protection.

The next day, the two men met him again and told the king that the
Muslims call Jesus the servant of God, and that he was a human being like
any other. The king once again summoned the Muslims to ask them about
what they would say about Jesus. The Muslims met together at night, and
they agreed to be truthful and tell the king what the Qur'an says about
Jesus. Again, Ja'far stood before the king and said: "We say what the
Prophet taught us: he is the servant of all, his messenger, and his spirit
and word he gave to Virgin Mary." The king picked a straw from the
ground, extended forward and said: "Jesus didn't exceed what you said
the magnitude of this straw."[1]

ALLIANCES

The companions' positive attitude toward the Abyssinian Christians
led to a strong and fruitful relationship for both. Not only did the friendly
relationship establish unbroken peace for over a millennium, but it also

---

[1]Ibn Hisham, *Al-Sirah Al-Nabawiyah* (Dar Al-Ma'rifah), p. 313.

helped the early Muslims stave off a serious economic boycott that threatened the emerging Muslim community. The strong alliance between the
Makkan Muslims and the Abyssinian Christians was documented in
two verses of Surah Qasas:

> Those to whom we sent the book before this—they do believe in this
> (revelation); and when it is recited to them, they say: We believe therein, for
> it is the truth from our Lord: indeed we have been Muslims (bowing to God's
> will) from before this. Twice will they be given their rewards, for that they
> have persevered, that they avert evil with good, and that they spend in char-
> ity out of what we have given them. And when they hear vain talk, they turn
> away there from and say: To us our deeds, and to you yours, peace be with
> you, we do not pursue the ignorant.
>
> (Qasas 28:52–55)

The above verses were revealed in reference to a Christian delegation
that was sent by Najashi to investigate the conditions of the Muslims in
Makkah, in the eighth year of revelation. Quraysh imposed an economic
and social boycott on the Prophet and Banu Hashim that lasted for
28 months, forcing them into an arid and narrow valley known as the
Abu-talib Valley. The boycott was harsh and severe and took its toll on
the Prophet and his family. The Prophet's wife, Khadijah, died in the
same year the boycott was ended, and shortly after her death, his Uncle
Abu Talib died.

There have been a number of accounts as to what triggered the lifting of
the boycott imposed by Quraysh on the Prophet's clan and his followers,
which lasted for three years. One report cites the wear and tear of the scroll
on which the boycott covenant was written; this scroll was hung on the
Sacred House. Another report attributes the nullification of the covenant
to the breakup of the alliance that was crucial for its enforcement. The fact,
though, is that the disagreement among Quraysh leaders took place
shortly after the King of Abyssinia sent, in collaboration with Ja'far bin
Abu Talib, a delegation of 33 Muslims and Christians to investigate the
conditions of the Muslims and their supporters.

COMMON GROUND

Therefore, the Muslim attitude towards the followers of other
religions, particularly the People of the Book, should not be one of self-
righteousness and pride but rather one of compassion, mutual respect,
and concern for the wellbeing and welfare of other communities. The
Qur'an encourages Muslims to cooperate for the common good and to
search for a common ground, based on mutual respect and help.

> Say: O People of the Book! Come to common terms as between us and you:
> that we worship none but God; that we associate no partners with him; that

we erect not, from among ourselves, lords and patrons other than God.
If then they turn back, say: Bear witness that we (at least) are Muslims
(bowing to God's will).

(Al 'Imran 3:94)

The common ground Muslims are asked to seek with the followers
of other religions is a society in which people are free to worship God.
In such open society Muslims must display a positive attitude and
unwavering respect for the followers of other faiths. Dealing with respect
and positive engagement does not mean that differences in doctrine and
interpretation do not matter. Rather, it means that those differences must
be addressed through free and open dialogue

Invite (all) to the way of your Lord with wisdom and beautiful preaching;
and argue with them in ways that are best and most gracious: for your Lord
knows best, who have strayed from his path, and who receive guidance.

(Nahl 16:125)

CHAPTER 25

Covenants and the Social Contract

Covenants and contracts are the most fundamental principles governing voluntary relationships among people. Covenants are solemn promises exchanged by individuals who have the intellectual, moral, and practical capacity to act on them. Contracts are, in contrast, legally binding agreements between parties to do or exchange certain things.

The Qur'an uses three distinct terms to refer to voluntary commitments and agreements: 'ahd (covenant), mithaq (pact), and 'aqd (contract). On the most basic level of meaning the three terms signify a mutual commitment to perform acts or services. The Qur'an, while underscoring the importance of fulfilling all commitments, uses the term "covenant" to denote the most solemn agreements, including agreements between human beings and the Divine; "pact" to refer to agreements among groups with internal solidarity; and "contract" for agreements subject to legal regulation and enforcement.

COVENANT WITH GOD

The covenant with God involves the exchange of promises between God and the human being, an agreement that binds the Divine and the human in a definitive relationship with certain expectations and consequences. The covenant, the Qur'an points out, preceded the act of human conception and creation and was solemnized with the expression of faith as humans reached their adulthood and maturation:

> Behold when your Lord drew forth from the children of Adam from their loins, their descendants, and made them testify concerning themselves, (saying): Am I not your Lord (who cherishes and sustains you)? They said: Yea! We do testify! (this), lest you should say on the day of judgment: Of this we were never mindful. Or lest you should say: Our fathers before us may

have taken false gods, but we are (their) descendants after them: will you
then destroy us because of the deeds of people who were futile?

(A'raf 7:172–173)

Exegesists differ as to whether the above verse should be understood
literally or figuratively, but the intended meaning is not in doubt: human
beings are created with an innate recognition of divinity and an innate
moral compass that guides humans towards what is good, right, peaceful,
and just. Humans cannot, therefore, absolve themselves from their spiritual, intellectual, and moral responsibilities.

O children of Israel! Call to mind the (special) favor which I bestowed upon
you, and fulfill your covenant with me as I fulfill my covenant with you,
and fear none but me.

(Baqarah 2:40)

The covenant between man and God at the moment of birth is intuitive
and instinctive, hence signifying the human capacity to recognize the
Divine. The covenant, however, takes a more solemn and demanding form
as people recognize the Divine and submit to the divine will as revealed
through scriptures and prophets. The children of Israel are reminded, in
the above verse, to maintain their promise to follow the divine will as a
precondition for receiving the promise that God gave them through
Prophet Musa (Moses). The children of Israel were required to obey God
and his commandments, and God would in return make them leaders in
this life and reward them with paradise in the life after.

It is the same covenant that all prophets, including Muhammad, the
Seal of Prophets, urged their people to observe and maintain.

What cause do you have not to believe in God? And the messenger invites
you to believe in your Lord, and has indeed taken your covenant, if you are
faithful.

(Hadid 57:8)

And so maintaining the covenant is the hallmark of true and sincere
faith. People of true faith will stay steadfastly committed to the universal
and transcendental values and principles demanded by the Divine, and
they will never waver in the face of adversity.

[The believers] fulfill the covenant of God and fail not in their plighted word.
(Ra'd 13:20)

Among the believers are men who have been true to their covenant with
God: of them some have completed their vow (to the extreme), and some
(still) wait: but they have never changed (their determination) in the least.
(Ahzab 33:23)

Wavering and breaking covenants are signs of hypocrisy and duplicity,
and they only lead to corruption and failure in this life and the hereafter.

Those who break God's covenant after it is ratified, and who sunder what God has ordered to be joined, and do mischief on earth: these cause losses (only) to themselves.

(Baqarah 2:27)

COVENANTS AND CONTRACTS AMONG PEOPLE

Keeping faith and staying true to one's covenants and commitments is expected in every aspect in life—including all relationships, not only in relation to one's obligations toward God. Honoring promises and contracts is emphatically demanded in the Qur'an:

O you who believe! Fulfill (all) obligations. Lawful unto you (for food) are all four-footed animals, with the exceptions named: but animals of the chase are forbidden while you are in the sacred precincts or in pilgrim garb: for God does command according to his will and plan.

(Ma'idah 5:1)

The believers, the Qur'an stresses, are always true to the promises they make and the contract they enter into. Contracts must be fulfilled, whether they involve business transactions, the marriage relationship, or promises to provide goods or services.

...those who faithfully observe their trusts and their covenants.

(Mu'minun 23:8)

But if you decide to take one wife in place of another, even if you had given the latter a whole treasure for dower, take not the least bit of it back; would you take it by slander and a manifest wrong? And how could you take it when you have gone in unto each other and they have taken from you a solemn covenant?

(Nisa' 4:20–21)

Come not nigh to the orphan's property except to improve it, until he attains the age of full strength; and fulfill (every) covenant, for (every) covenant will be enquired into (on the day of reckoning).

(Isra' 17:34)

To ensure that contracts are based on clear understanding and are protected, the Qur'an requires the believers to write all their agreements, regardless of whether the agreement has little or great significance.

O you who believe! When you deal with each other, in transactions involving future obligations in a fixed period of time, reduce them to writing and let a scribe write down faithfully as between the parties; let not the scribe refuse to write: as God has taught him, so let him write. Let him who incurs the liability dictate, but let him fear his Lord God, and not diminish aught of what he owes. ...Disdain not to reduce to writing (your contract) for a future period, whether it be small or big: it is more just in the sight of God, more suitable as evidence, and more convenient to prevent doubts among yourselves but if it be a transaction which you carry out on the spot among yourselves there is no blame on you if you reduce it not to writing. But bring witnesses whenever you make a commercial contract; and let neither the scribe nor the witness suffer harm. If you do (such harm), then it would be wickedness in you. So fear God; for it is God that teaches you. And God is well acquainted with all things.

(Baqarah 2:282)

SOCIAL CONTRACT ABOVE RELIGIOUS SOLIDARITY

Perhaps the most important covenant, after the covenant with God, is the social covenant that establishes peace and cooperation between peoples and groups with varying religious, tribal, ethnic, and racial backgrounds. Covenants among groups create solemn obligations that surpass all other human covenants and obligations, including the obligation to show solidarity to members of the faith.

Those who believed and migrated, and fought in the way (required) by God, with their property and their persons, as well as those who gave (them) asylum and aid, these are (all) friends and protectors, one of another. As to those who believed but have not yet immigrated; you owe no duty of protection to them until they migrate; but if they seek your aid in religion, it is your duty to help them, except against a people with whom you have a treaty of mutual covenant. And (remember) God sees all that you do.

(Anfal 8:72)

Establishing social covenants that defined the rights and duties of the members of the social groups forming the polity of Medina was the first act of the Prophet upon moving from Makkah to Medina. The covenant did not impose Islamic religious values on Medinan society; rather it established a multireligious and pluralist social order based on universally valid principles. The Compact of Medina was the first written political document that we are aware of that established political freedoms and rights, including the freedom of religion. Therefore, contrary to the claims of both Muslim extremists and their counterparts in the Christian and Jewish communities, Islam and Islamic law do not call for the imposition of Islamic values and teachings on the followers of the other religions. "This is a covenant given by Muhammad to the believers and the Muslims of Quraysh, Yathrib, and those who followed them, joined them, and fought with them. They constitute one *ummah* to the exclusion of all others....Any Jew who follows us is entitled to our assistance and the same rights as any one of us, without injustice or partisanship."[1]

The covenant goes on to recognize the religious freedom of the parties of the covenant and ensure the equal dignity of all.

---

[1]Ibn Hisham, *Al-Sirah Al-Nabawiyah* (Dar Al-Kunuz Al-Adabiyah), vol. 2, p. 501–502.

The Jews have their religion and the Muslims theirs. Both enjoy the security of their own populace and alliances (*mawali*) except the unjust and the criminal among them. . . . Each must help the other against anyone who attacks the people of this Compact. They must seek mutual advice and consultation.

To the Jew who follows us belongs help and equality. He shall not be wronged nor shall his enemies be aided.[2]

The town of Yathrib shall constitute a sanctuary for the parties of this covenant. Their neighbors shall be treated as themselves as long as they perpetrate no crime and commit no harm.[3]

The covenant stipulated that the social and political activities in the new system must be subject to a set of universal values and standards that treat all people equally. Sovereignty in the society would not rest with the rulers, nor any particular group, but with the law founded on the basis of justice and goodness, maintaining the dignity of all. The compact emphasized repeatedly and frequently the fundamentality of justice, goodness, and righteousness, and it condemned in different expressions injustice and tyranny. "They would redeem their prisoners with kindness and justice common among the believers," the compact stated. "The God-conscious believers shall be against the rebellious, and against those who seek to spread injustice, sin, enmity, or corruption among the believers, the hand of every person shall be against him even if he be a son of one of them," it proclaimed.[4]

The covenant introduced a number of political rights to be enjoyed by the individuals of the Medinan State, Muslims and non-Muslims alike, including (1) the obligation to help the oppressed; (2) outlawing guilt by association, which was commonly practiced by pre-Islamic Arab tribes: "A person is not liable for his ally's misdeeds"; (3) freedom of belief: "The Jews have their religion and the Muslims theirs"; and (4) freedom of movement from and to Medina: "Whoever will go out is safe, and whoever will stay in Medina is safe except those who wronged (others), or committed offense."[5]

---

[2]Ibn Hisham, *Al-Sirah Al-Nabawiyah* (Dar Al-Kunuz Al-Adabiyah), vol. 2, p. 501–502.
[3]Ibid.
[4]Ibid.
[5]Ibid.

PART VI

ETERNAL PEACE

Eternal peace marks the conclusion of the struggle to realize peace. Eternal peace is the goal of all human spirits that are aware of their transient life and who, hence, long to find their fulfillment in eternal life. This fulfillment must await the moment of death. And here lies the paradox of death: a moment that seemingly repudiates life is the precondition for eternal life and eternal peace. In the struggle to realize eternal peace, the faithful learn not only to accept death but to welcome it, as the reaffirmation of life in its broadest and deepest sense.

CHAPTER 26

Life and Death

Life and death are intertwined in human experience. The life of any human being is delineated by two points in time, birth and death: a person comes to life at the moment of birth and leaves it at the moment of death. Visiting a graveyard, one can identify the buried by their names and the dates of birth and death that are usually engraved on the headstones of their graves.

STATE OF BEING

The life of a person in its simplest manifestation is associated with the person's physical presence, with his or her bodily motions—in the ability to move muscles, eat, drink, or breathe. When these basic functions stop, and the human body becomes irresponsive, the person is pronounced dead, his body is disposed of, and the person disappears.

The human presence on earth is surrounded by two periods of absence: one precedes his or her birth and the other succeeds it. The Qur'an refers to the two time spans that precede and succeed individual lives as "death."

> How can you reject the faith in God? Seeing that you were without life, and he gave you life; then will he cause you to die, and will again bring you to life; and again to him will you return.
>
> (Baqarah 2:28)

Death is presented here as a state and not an event. It is associated with the absence of life and of consciousness. Human life succeeds a state of death and is in turn succeeded by a second state of death, before the eternal life ensues when the human being returns to God. The notion that the human being emanates from God and then returns to him is stated clearly in the Qur'an:

Those who [are patient] say, when afflicted with calamity: To God we belong,
and to him is our return.

(Baqarah 2:156)

Death is the absence of consciousness and effectiveness, and it
surrounds human life. Human beings come to life from a state in which
they lack both consciousness and effectiveness and then return to it
temporarily, before they are brought back to an eternal life. The Qur'anic
notion of death becomes more interesting when we realize that death
does not only precede and succeed individual life, but it permeates it as
well. Indeed, the Qur'an refers to the absence of consciousness during
sleep as a state of temporary death. For in both cases, God "recalls" the
human being back into a state in which the human being is oblivious to
the world:

It is God that recalls the souls at death; and those that die not (he recalls)
during their sleep: those on whom he has passed the decree of death, he
keeps back (from returning to life), but the rest he sends (to their bodies)
for a term appointed. Verily in this are signs for those who reflect.

(Zumar 39:42)

The mystery of life and death is approached metaphorically in the
Qur'an. The notion of the returning vegetation to a dead earth, that is, to
the desert that has been stripped of all vegetation after a long, dry summer,
is the metaphor that the Qur'an frequently uses to illustrate the succession
of life and death:

It is he who brings out the living from the dead, and brings out the dead from
the living, and who gives life to the earth after it is dead: and thus shall you
be brought out (from the dead).

(Rum 30:22)

Then contemplate the memorials of God's mercy! How he gives life to the
earth after its death: verily the same will give life to the humans who are
dead: for he has power over all things

(Rum 30:50)

The return of vegetation to the desert during the brief rainy season is a
resurrection of a sort. For here one can vividly observe how the green
color of grass and small plants emerges from the golden sand shortly after
heavy rain pours from the sky. The resurrection of human beings does not
take place as a result of heavy rain, but rather it has to wait for a moment
of time after all forms of life disappear from the face of the earth. At that
moment every human soul who ever lived will return to life in preparation for the day of judgment.

The trumpet shall be sounded, when behold! From the graves (people) will
rush forth to their Lord!

(Yasin 36:51)

Still, the mystery of life and death is recounted in the state of those who die upholding the commandments of God and his way, those who die while defending the principles of right, goodness, justice, and truth. Their experience of death will be markedly different than the one experienced by others:

> And say not of those who are slain in the way of God: They are dead. Nay, they are living, though you perceive (it) not.
>
> (Baqarah 2:154)

The death of the martyr is no more the absence of consciousness but rather a life more pronounced than the life of the living. With the death of a martyr the concept of time breaks down. Death is no longer a stage that succeeds the earthly life in preparation for the return to life on the day of resurrection, but rather it becomes a continuation of life in a different form. This continued awareness and heightened state of consciousness of the martyr is illustrated in Surah Yasin. The Qur'an narrates the story of a man who challenged his people when they decided to kill the three messengers that were sent to them to convey the divine message. He was himself put to death along with them, and here is what the Qur'an relates as to his afterlife experience:

> It was said: Enter you the garden. He said: Ah me! Would that my people knew (what I know)! For that my Lord has granted me forgiveness and has enrolled me among those held in honor!
>
> (Yasin 36:26–27)

The death of the righteous man in the above verse is presented as a step from an earthly life to the eternal life of bliss—a revolving door that instantaneously takes him from one state to another. On the level of human awareness and consciousness, death is the absence of consciousness; hence no matter how long it is, an absence of consciousness, whether sleep or death, passes in no time. This is true for both the martyr and the wrongdoer, as the Qur'an points out:

> The trumpet shall be sounded, when behold! From the graves people will rush forth to their Lord! They will say: Ah! Woe unto us! Who has raised us up from our beds of repose? (A voice will say) This is what (God) most compassionate had promised, and true was the word of the messengers!
>
> (Yasin 36:51–52)

For an unconscious person, it does not matter whether the time of death (or that of sleep, for that matter) is an hour or a million years—the distance between the moments of death and resurrection appears so close that one would experience resurrection at the moment of death. In Surah 30, the Qur'an narrates the state of mind of those who rejected faith when they are brought back to life. Their time of death would feel like a brief moment:

On the day that the hour (of reckoning) will be established, the transgressors will swear that they tarried not but an hour: thus were they used to being deluded! But those endued with knowledge and faith will say: Indeed you did tarry, within God's decree, to the day of resurrection, and this is the day of resurrection: but you were not aware!

(Rum 30:55–56)

TIMELESS LIFE

In addition to the temporal definition of life and death, the Qur'an introduces a different, and to a great extent, a counterintuitive definition of life. In the Qur'anic conceptualization of life and death, time limitations and contemporaneous motions lose their significance, and human presence becomes paramount.

The most striking encounter with this timeless and counterintuitive meaning of life and death can be found in Surah Fatir, where the Qur'an asserts the inequality between the state of life and the state of death:

Nor are they alike, those that are living and those that are dead. God can make any that he wills to hear; but you cannot make those to hear who are buried in graves.

(Fatir 35:22)

Given the context of this statement, it is clear that the Qur'an gives preference to the living over the dead. On its face value, the assertion seems a sensible celebration of life and a recognition that a living person is more precious to another living being. After all, one cannot speak to the dead in their graves and expect them to hear and respond. On a second thought, the statement becomes troubling if taken literally. For this literal meaning would imply that all living persons are better than all dead persons. But this cannot be the intended meaning of the Qur'anic verse, since it would imply that a reckless person, a mass murderer, or a tyrant who lives today is better than prophets, great leaders, scientists, or innovators who lived in the past.

The only way for the above verse to be interpreted in a manner consistent with the Qur'anic outlook is to recognize that the living and the dead are not referenced here in any temporal sense. The Qur'an asserts in the verse that life and death transcend time and space. The Qur'an talks here about living people who are, for all practical purposes, dead, and dead people who are alive. A person who died a long time ago, but whose legacy continues to impact human life today, is far more involved in nurturing human life than a living person whose life adds nothing to the value and meaning of collective humanity—even worse if his or her life takes away from the collective life and makes a negative contribution to the totality.

This meaning becomes evident when we examine other verses that stress the importance of responding to the call on humanity to live up to the high moral values demanded by divine revelation. Responding positively to the divine call, the Qur'an asserts, invigorates life and enriches it.

> O you who believe! Give your response to God and his messenger, when he calls you to that which will give you life; and know that God comes in between man and his heart, and that it is he to whom you shall all be gathered.
>
> (Anfal 8:24)

Failing to respond to human needs, to rise above immediate self-gratification, and to live a moral life reveals a state of being in which the life of the individual is as good in the greater scheme of things as the absence of life.

> Those who listen (in truth), be sure, will respond. As to the dead, God will raise them up, then will they be turned unto him.
>
> (An'am 6:36)

People who fail to relate to the world in a responsible way, to contribute positively to improving the world around themselves, add nothing with their presence to the life around them; so their presence and absence are of equal weight.

A person who, on the other hand, decides to engage the world in ways that will enhance life, by extending his or her personal skills and resources toward the benefit of other human beings, transforms their lives profoundly and makes his or her presence felt in positive and constructive ways beyond that person's immediate life.

> Can he who was dead, to whom we gave life, and a light whereby he can walk amongst men, be like him who is in the depths of darkness, from which he can never come out? Thus to those without faith their own deeds seem pleasing.
>
> (An'am 6:122)

> Truly you cannot cause the dead to listen, nor can you cause the deaf to hear the call, (especially) when they turn back in retreat. Nor can you be a guide to the blind, (to prevent them) from straying; only those will listen who believe in our signs, and they will bow in Islam.
>
> (Naml 27:80–81)

As the person who is physically irresponsive is declared dead, so a person who is morally or socially irresponsive to individuals and events around himself or herself should be considered lifeless.

Considering the new insights into death provided by the Qur'an, the event of death that marks the end of earthly life makes life more pointed and focused. The fear of death is no more fear of the conclusion of earthly life but rather the fear of wasting life in ways that make the life and death, or presence and absence, of a person of the same order. Death should never be feared but instead be anticipated, so as to make people want to measure their lives by their depth rather than their length.

CHAPTER 27

Salvation and Divine Judgment

Salvation, being saved from suffering and delivered from anguish, is instinctively desired by human beings. No body desires pain, and no one requires anguish. Human beings seek joy and happiness and desire a life of fulfillment and bliss. While no human being can escape pain and suffering of a sort in this life, most people are content with a life that is a mixture of joy and pain. Some though, are more blessed than others with a life of fulfillment, plenty, and joy.

But what about an eternal life in which a person is destined to a life of either full bliss and joy, or utter pain and suffering? This is a prospect that is both exuberating and horrifying—exuberating to anticipate an eternal life of bliss and horrifying to think of an eternal doom. Yet these are the very prospects anticipated by the divine revelation brought by the prophets of transcendence, and these are the prospects presented in the Qur'an.

Believing in a life after death, and in a life of either eternal reward or endless punishment, is a fundamental article of faith in the Qur'an. No article of faith is as much demanded in the Qur'anic revelation after the belief of the oneness of God than belief in the day of judgment. The Qur'an teaches that earthly life is short and temporary, and that it is intended for trial and test in preparation for an eternal life. Death is not the end of human life but the beginning of a more profound, consequential, and lasting life. The quality of the eternal life hinges, though, on the choices human beings make in the earthly life. Eternal salvation lies in attaining a position in paradise that brings the individual closer to God, while eternal doom is felt by those who are pushed away from the Divine into hell.

Coming back to life on a day when every human being that has ever lived is resurrected, to face his or her life work and to take responsibility for statements and actions that were said and done during the earthly life, is what the revelation refers to as the day of resurrection (*yawm al-qiyamah*), the day of judgment (*yawm al-hisab*), or simply the "final day" (*al-yawm al-akhir*).

Resurrection, eternal salvation, the pleasure of God, the exuberance of paradise, and the horror of hell have forever elicited both hope and fear. The questions of what the Qur'an has to say on these issues, and of what sense one can derive from these concepts, are the focus of this chapter.

DAY OF JUDGMENT

The earthly life is a temporary life for both the individual human being and humanity at large. The earthly life of the individual culminates with death, while the earthly life of the entire human race ends with the final day:

> No just estimate have they made of God, such as is due to him: on the day of judgment the whole of the earth will be but his handful, and the heavens will be rolled up in his right hand: glory to him! High is he above the partners they attribute to him! The trumpet will (just) be sounded, when all that are in the heavens and on earth will swoon, except such as it will please God (to exempt). Then will a second one be sounded, when, behold, they will be standing and looking on!
>
> (Zumar 39:67–68)

Life on earth will end with a trumpet-like sound that will make every living being collapse in shock, practically ending the first phase of human life. This will be followed with a similar sound that brings every human being that ever lived to life again to witness the greatest gathering of all, the gathering of humanity to experience the divine promise of accountability and an eternal life of either felicity or anguish.

Between the two trumpet-like sounds that mark the end of the short earthly life and the beginning of eternal life lie cataclysmic events of cosmic proportions. The Qur'an describes these events in terms that suggest redesign and recreation of the entire universe:

> The day that we roll up the heavens like a scroll rolled up, so as we started the first creation, so shall we bring a new one: a promise we have undertaken: truly shall we fulfill it.
>
> (Anbiya' 21:104)

Humans will return to life in a universe that is completely different from the one they encountered in their mortal life:

One day the earth will be changed to a different earth, and so will be the heavens, and (humans) will be marshaled forth, before God, the One, the Irresistible.

(Ibrahim 41:48)

Not only will the natural order look and feel different, but human senses and perception will undergo a drastic change. For one, the ability of people to observe reality and respond to stimulation will be sharply different:

And the trumpet shall be blown: that will be the day whereof warning (had been given). And there will come forth every soul: with each will be an (angel) to drive, and an (angel) to bear witness. (It will be said:) You were heedless of this, now have we removed your veil, and sharp is your sight this day!

(Qaf 50:20–22)

The sharpness of vision and sight will be overwhelming, particularly for those who thought they would never have to account for their earthly choices and deeds. For the record is detailed and complete, so much so that nothing seems to escape from it:

And the book (of deeds) will be placed (before you); and you will see the sinful in great terror because of what is (recorded) therein; they will say, Ah! woe to us! what a book is this! it leaves out nothing small or great, but takes account thereof! They will find all that they did placed before them: and not one will your Lord treat with injustice.

(Kahf 18:49)

THE ORDER OF TRUTH AND JUSTICE

Human beings, the Qur'an asserts, were created to play an important role in the universe. They have been empowered to inhabit and take charge of the most colorful planet in the universe. The mission they have is a collective mission, and to achieve it effectively and appropriately, they are expected to treat each other fairly and to take care of each other's rights and needs.

The day of judgment will split, as it were, human life into two phases: mortal and eternal. The mortal phase is afflicted with suffering, conflict, and limitation of resources; the eternal phase is characterized by harmony, fulfillment, and plenty. The Qur'an does not elaborate as to whether humans will have a different mission in the hereafter, but it is clear that the quality of life will undergo drastic, even breathtaking, change. For here humanity will be divided into the people of paradise and those of hell.

Dividing humanity between paradise and hell is depicted in the Qur'an as inevitable, required by the very qualities of the Divine, by the qualities of mercy, justice, and faithfulness.

> Say: To whom belongs all that is in the heavens and on earth? Say: To God.
> He has inscribed for himself (the rule of) mercy. That he will gather you
> together for the day of judgment, there is no doubt whatever. It is they who
> have lost their own souls, that will not believe.
>
> (An'am 6:12)

It is not quite apparent, and might be counterintuitive to many, as to
how the day of judgment could be a sign of divine mercy, when the outcome of that day will set a significant number of human beings on a
course to eternal suffering and anguish. The judgment is so grave and
the calculations are so complex that humans may not be able to appreciate
all aspects of the divine judgment.

What is clear, though, is that the prospects of eternal felicity and
anguish have been essential for developing moral discipline for countless
individuals and communities. Every human civilization the world has
witnessed has been founded on a religious foundation. And in all world
religions, the question of universal human responsibility before the Divine
has been central in the religious consciousness of people.

Still, despite warnings and threats of grievous consequences, there are
those who have rebelled against divine guidance and indulged themselves in excesses and injustice. The Qur'an presents divine punishment
as the inevitable consequence of the dispensation of justice.

> We shall set up scales of justice for the day of judgment, so that not a soul will
> be dealt with unjustly in the least. And if there be (no more than) the weight
> of a mustard seed, we will bring it (to account): and enough are we to take
> account.
>
> (Anbiya' 21:47)

Divine justice will be based on precise measures and scales, and no one
will escape the demands of justice. There will be no extraneous appeal or
intercession, just the demands of justice.

> Then guard yourselves against a day when one soul shall not avail another
> nor shall intercession be accepted for her, nor shall compensation be taken
> from her, nor shall anyone be helped (from outside).
>
> (Baqarah 2:48)

The sense of inevitability that leads to the segregation of people
between paradise and hell is always evident in the Qur'an. It is a fulfillment of divine justice, knowledge, wisdom, and design. The word that
brings about such consequences is already out, and it is a divine word
that can only be based on deliberation and completeness, away from
human compulsiveness and haste.

> If we had so willed, we could certainly have brought every soul its true guid-
> ance: but the word from me will come true, I will fill hell with *jinns* and
> humans all together.
>
> (Sajdah 32:13)

The segregation, though, is far from being capricious or arbitrary. It based on clear criteria. Those whose abode will be hellfire are arrogant, mean, stubborn; and those who will be granted paradise are those who have been distinguished with good will and deeds.

> Throw, throw into hell every contumacious rejecter, (of God)! Who forbade what was good, transgressed all bounds, cast doubts and suspicions; who set up another god beside God: throw him into a severe penalty. His companion will say: Our Lord! I did not make him transgress, but he was (himself) far astray. He will say: Dispute not with each other in my presence: I had already in advance sent you warning. One day we will ask hell: Are you filled to the full? It will say: Are there any more (to come)? And the garden will be brought nigh to the righteous; no more a thing distant. (A voice will say:) This is what was promised for you, for everyone who turned (to God) in sincere repentance, who kept (his law), who feared (God) Most Gracious unseen, and brought a heart turned in devotion (to him): enter you therein in peace and security; this is a day of eternal life! There will be for them therein all that they wish, and more besides in our presence.
>
> (Qaf 50:24–34)

The like of those who are destined to hell are people who persecuted fellow human beings for no fault other than choosing a life of faith and truth.

> Those who persecute (or draw into temptation) the believers, men and women, and do not turn in repentance, will have the penalty of hell: they will have the penalty of the burning fire.
>
> (Buruj 85:10)

Anyone who chose goodness over evil and displayed faith in God will be rewarded with paradise.

> If any do deeds of righteousness—be they male or female—and have faith, they will enter heaven, and not the least injustice will be done to them.
>
> (Nisa' 4:124)

Of course people are not, and should never be seen as, as either purely good or purely evil. People have mixed packages of both and sometimes effect evil outcomes even when they intend good. So the question is whether humans are aware of their moral limitations and are working to improve them through repentance and discipline—or whether they are arrogant, reckless, and irresponsible and hence are stubborn in their pursuit of their selfish ends. It is the latter who are described in the Qur'an as rebellious (*kufr*) and who set themselves up on a path for eternal anguish.

BETWEEN PARADISE AND HELL

Paradise and hell are not spiritual states but will be experienced, the Qur'an stresses, both physically and spiritually, whereby people will have experiences not unlike those encountered in the earthly life. The Qur'an suggests that people will undergo a physiological transformation of sorts in order to accord with the new life situation. This transformation may be similar to the one the first human beings, Adam and Eve, experienced after they ate of the forbidden fruit and became aware of their private parts, of which they were not at all aware, or not vividly aware, before.

The Qur'an is full of passages that provide glimpses of the eternal life in paradise and hell. In Chapter 39, otherwise known as Surah Zumar, the Qur'an fast-forwards the reader to the moment when people are led by the angels to their places of eternal dwelling, describing instances of emotions and conversations:

> And the earth will shine with the glory of its Lord: the record (of deeds) will be placed (open); the prophets and the witnesses will be brought forward; and a just decision pronounced between them; and they will not be wronged (in the least). And to every soul will be paid in full (the fruit) of its deeds; and (God) knows best all that they do. The unbelievers will be led to hell in crowd: until, when they arrive there, its gates will be opened. And its keepers will say: Did not messengers come to you from among yourselves, rehearsing to you the signs of your Lord, and warning you of the meeting of this day of yours? The answer will be: True: but the decree of punishment has been proved true against the unbelievers! (To them) will be said: Enter the gates of hell, to dwell therein: and evil is (this) abode of the arrogant! And those who feared their Lord will be led to the garden in crowds: until behold, they arrive there; its gates will be opened; and its keepers will say: Peace be upon you! Well have you done! Enter here, to dwell therein. They will say: Praise be to God, who has truly fulfilled his promise to us, and has given us (this) land in heritage: we can dwell in the garden as we will: how excellent a reward for those who work (righteousness)! And you will see the angels surrounding the throne (divine) on all sides, singing glory and praise to their Lord. The decision between them (at judgment) will be in (perfect) justice, and the cry (on all sides) will be, Praise be to God, the Lord of the Worlds!
>
> (Zumar 39:69–75)

The experience in the hereafter recalls many aspects of the earthly life. It involves feelings of pleasure and pain, of fulfillment and disappointment, and of intellectual and emotional awareness. The obvious difference is that the overall setting is overwhelmingly skewed in one way or the other. People in the life to come will experience either thorough and unhindered joy and fulfillment or utter pain and disappointment. People will also experience a universe that is more transparent and open to human senses, beyond anything they experienced in this life. The Qur'an talks about an experience of the presence of the angels and the throne, that is the divine seat, a notion that human beings can hardly start to comprehend here and now.

The intellectual and emotional experiences of the people in the life hereafter are not only communicated among the dwellers of one abode or the other. They will, in fact, be communicated across the divide that separates the peoples of paradise and of hell. The divide, as described by the Qur'an, while transparent, is rigid and impenetrable. People across the divide will be able to see and communicate but unable to change conditions and situations.

The Qur'an provides examples of conversations between the angels and the dwellers of paradise and hell, as well as the exchange that will take place between the dwellers themselves.

> The companions of the garden will call out to the companions of the fire: We have indeed found the promises of our Lord to us true: have you also found your Lord's promises true? They shall say, Yes; but a crier shall proclaim between them: The curse of God is on the wrongdoers. Those who would hinder (men) from the path of God and would seek in it something crooked: they were those who denied the hereafter. Between them shall be a veil, and on the heights will be men who would know everyone by his marks: they will call out to the companions of the garden, Peace on you: they will not have entered, but they will have an assurance (thereof). When their eyes shall be turned towards the companions of the fire, they will say: Our Lord! Send us not to the company of the wrongdoers. The men on the heights will call to certain men whom they will know from their marks, saying: Of what profit to you were your hoards and your arrogant ways? Behold! Are these not the men whom you swore that God with his mercy would never bless? Enter you the garden: no fear shall be on you, nor shall you grieve. The companions of the fire will call to the companions of the garden: Pour down to us water or anything that God does provide for your sustenance. They will say: Both these things has God forbidden to those who rejected him. Such as took their religion to be mere amusement and play, and were deceived by the life of the world. That day shall we forget them as they forgot the meeting of this day of theirs, and as they were wont to reject our signs.
>
> (A'raf 7:44–51)

There is still hope for the people of hell, as some of them will escape their miserable conditions after spending the amount of time that fit their crimes. Those, however, who showed complete arrogance, denied the truth, and rejected the call to live a life of peace and justice will be consigned to hell, never getting near to paradise.

> To those who reject our signs and treat them with arrogance, no opening will there be of the gates of heaven, nor will they enter the garden, until the camel can pass through the eye of the needle: such is our reward for those in sin.
>
> (A'raf 7:40)

> God forgives not that partners should be set up with him; but he forgives anything else, to whom he pleases; to set up partners with God is to devise a sin most heinous indeed.
>
> (Nisa' 4:48)

Those, on the other hand, who were granted paradise will dwell therein not for years or centuries but for eternity, and they will remain there as long as the newly structured heavens and the earth persist.

> And those who are blessed shall be in the garden: they will dwell therein for all the time that the heavens and the earth endure, except as your Lord wills: a gift without break.

> (Hud 11:108)

SALVATION

Salvation is for the righteous, and God alone will decide who will be saved in the life to come; this is the clear pronouncement of the Qur'an. In infinite divine wisdom, God decided that this life of conflict and suffering is the prelude to an eternal life of fulfillment and endless possibilities. He also made true faith, good intentions, and good deeds the means through which humans can grow morally, spiritually, and socially and become more deserving of salvation and forgiveness.

While struggle and endeavors are the prelude to salvation, God's mercy alone can save people. No human being could enter paradise if the principles of justice alone were to be applied. It is divine grace and forgiveness that overlook the shortcomings and failings of people and that redeem in the life to come. Yet divine justice will be the imperative that will cast those who were committed to a life of injustice, excess, and arrogance to hell. The merciful, compassionate, loving, and caring Divine is also a just Divine, whose justice will be on display for all to see and experience.

Yet it is not up to people to assume the divine role and pass judgment on others. No human being is equipped to decipher the mystery of life and the human will. Only God can justly judge people. Indeed, on the day of judgment, certain people who were judged as evil by their fellow human beings will be saved by the all-knowing and all-merciful God.

> And they will say: What has happened to us that we see not men whom we used to number among the bad ones? Did we treat them (as such) in ridicule, or have (our) eyes failed to perceive them? Truly that is just and fitting, the mutual recriminations of the people of the fire!

> (Sad 38:62–64)

Transient and finite humans, who have limited knowledge and compassion, are naturally biased in their judgment, and hence they cannot always render a fair judgment. Humans are biased by their own particular time, gender, ethnicity, circumstances, and those who are good to them. God, and God alone, is the final arbiter and judge, and for that all humans must be grateful.

Epilogue:
Readers and Travelers

Life and death, faith and infidelity, truth and falsehood, peace and war, infinity and finitude, confidence and arrogance, moderation and excess, hope and despair, good and evil, justice and oppression, compassion and intolerance, love and greed—these are words and themes that permeate the Qur'anic message. They serve as triggers that ignite the powerful energy that constitutes the human spirit. Whether the spiritual energy of the human being is transformed into burning heat or guiding light is a question of interpretation and order.

The impact of words and verses ultimately hinges on how the words are ordered and verses are interpreted. It hinges on the extent to which the meaning derived from the revealed source is partial or complete. Partial meanings release partial and imbalanced energy, turning the revealed words into a source of destructive energy that burns all who come near them, while complete meanings shine brilliantly, enlightening all who are drawn to them.

Yet partial reading, interpretation, and application are outer signs of deeper problems concerning human will and purpose. They reflect a concealed desire to subordinate truths to personal gains, instead of aligning one's will to transcendental will and sublime purposes and values. Partial reading, as the Qur'an puts it, indicates ill intent.

> He it is who has sent down to you the book; in it are verses of profound meaning; they are the foundation of the book: others are not of well-established meaning. But those in whose hearts is perversity follow the part thereof that is not of well-established meaning, seeking discord and alternation, but no one knows its true meanings except God. And those who are firmly grounded in knowledge say: We believe in the book; the whole of it is from our Lord; and none will grasp the message except people of understanding.
>
> (Al 'Imran 3:7)

The received message is not simply a question of text but of context as well. Its meaning is not completely subsumed in the meaning intended in the source but also depends on the meaning derived by the reader. Meaning also depends on the recipients of the message, on their intentions and circumstances. It matters a great deal whether the recipients of the message and the readers of the divine text are willing to submit their individual and particular wills to transcendental truth and law, or whether they want to manipulate the message to privilege their individual interests and limited aims over universal principles and transcendental law.

The Qur'an is, indeed, susceptible to many readings, and it has been read in many ways. The content and style of the book leave no doubts that it was intended as an open and dynamic message. It was intended to address human intelligence, spark noble emotions, and inspire people by awakening their spiritual energy. And so if people are diverse in their purposes and experience, so must be their readings of the revealed book and their understanding of the intended message.

And as it was true when the Qur'an was revealed, it is still true today, that certain readers of the revealed words are intent on pursuing the perplexing verses, while they cast aside the most profound and foundational verses. The journey we undertook in this book into the main themes of the Qur'an should convince any open-minded traveler that its message is grounded in the sublime moral teachings that inspired, and continue to inspire, countless people to live a life of service, compassion, dignity, and courage.

APPENDIX A

Surahs of the Qur'an

The Qur'an comprises 114 surahs (chapters) and 6,236 ayahs (verses), containing 99,464 words.

Below is a summary of the surahs of the Qur'an numbered in the order they appear. The table also shows the city in which various surahs were revealed and the number of verses that are comprised in each.

Surah No.	Name of Surah (Arabic)	Name of Surah (English)	City of Revelation	Number of Verses
1	Fatihah	Opening*	Makkah	7
2	Baqarah	Cow	Medina	286
3	Al 'Imran	House of Imran	Medina	200
4	Nisa'	Women	Medina	176
5	Ma'idah	Table	Medina	120
6	An'am	Cattle	Makkah	165
7	A'raf	Embankments	Makkah	206
8	Anfal	Spoils	Medina	75
9	Tawbah	Repentance	Medina	129
10	Yunus	Jonah	Makkah	109
11	Hud	Hud	Makkah	123
12	Yusuf	Joseph	Makkah	111
13	Ra'd	Thunder	Medina	43
14	Ibrahim	Abraham	Makkah	52
15	Hijr	Chamber	Makkah	99
16	Nahl	Bee	Makkah	128
17	Isra'	Night Journey	Makkah	111

18	Kahf	Cave	Makkah	110
19	Maryam	Mary	Makkah	98
20	Taha	Taha	Makkah	135
21	Anbiya'	Prophets	Makkah	112
22	Hajj	Pilgrimage	Medina	78
23	Mu'minun	Believers	Makkah	118
24	Nur	Light	Makkah	64
25	Furqan	Salvation	Makkah	77
26	Shu'ara'	Poets	Makkah	227
27	Naml	Ant	Makkah	93
28	Qasas	Story	Makkah	88
29	'Ankabut	Spider	Makkah	69
30	Rum	Romans	Makkah	60
31	Luqman	Lokman	Makkah	34
32	Sajdah	Prostration	Makkah	30
33	Ahzab	Confederates	Medina	73
34	Saba'	Sheba	Makkah	54
35	Fatir	Originator	Makkah	45
36	Yasin	Yasin	Makkah	83
37	Saffat	Rangers	Makkah	182
38	Sad	Saad	Makkah	88
39	Zumar	Companies	Makkah	75
40	Ghafir	Forgiver	Makkah	85
41	Fussilat	Detailed	Makkah	54
42	Shura	Counsel	Makkah	53
43	Zukhruf	Ornaments	Makkah	89
44	Dukhan	Smoke	Makkah	59
45	Jathiyah	Hobbling	Makkah	37
46	Ahqaf	Sand Dunes	Makkah	35
47	Muhammad	Muhammad	Medina	38
48	Fath	Victory	Medina	29
49	Hujurat	Apartments	Medina	18
50	Qaf	Qaf	Makkah	45
51	Dhariyat	Scatterers	Makkah	60
52	Tur	The Mount	Makkah	49

53	Najm	Star	Makkah	62
54	Qamar	Moon	Makkah	55
55	Rahman	Merciful	Medina	78
56	Waqi'ah	Event	Makkah	96
57	Hadid	Iron	Medina	29
58	Mujadilah	Disputer	Medina	22
59	Hashr	Mustering	Medina	24
60	Mumtahinah	Tested Woman	Medina	13
61	Saff	Ranks	Medina	14
62	Jumu'ah	Congregation	Medina	11
63	Munafiqun	Hypocrites	Medina	11
64	Taghabun	Mutual Fraud	Medina	18
65	Talaq	Divorce	Medina	12
66	Tahrim	Forbidding	Medina	12
67	Mulk	Kingdom	Makkah	30
68	Qalam	Pen	Makkah	52
69	Haqqah	Indubitable	Makkah	52
70	Ma'arij	Stairways	Makkah	44
71	Nuh	Noah	Makkah	28
72	Jinn	Jinn	Makkah	28
73	Muzammil	Enwrapped	Makkah	20
74	Mudaththir	Shrouded	Makkah	56
75	Qiyamah	Resurrection	Makkah	40
76	Insan	Man	Makkah	31
77	Mursalat	Emissaries	Makkah	50
78	Naba'	Tiding	Makkah	40
79	Nazi'at	Pluckers	Makkah	46
80	'Abasa	Frowned	Makkah	42
81	Takwir	Rounding	Makkah	29
82	Infitar	Splitting	Makkah	19
83	Mutaffifin	Stinters	Makkah	36
84	Inshiqaq	Rending	Makkah	25
85	Buruj	Constellations	Makkah	22
86	Tariq	Night Star	Makkah	17
87	A'la	Most High	Makkah	19

88	Ghashiyah	Enveloper	Makkah	26
89	Fajr	Dawn	Makkah	30
90	Balad	Town	Makkah	20
91	Shams	Sun	Makkah	15
92	Layl	Night	Makkah	21
93	Duha	Forenoon	Makkah	11
94	Inshirah	Expanding	Makkah	8
95	Tin	Fig	Makkah	8
96	'Alaq	Blood Clot	Makkah	19
97	Qadr	Power	Makkah	5
98	Bayyinah	Clear Sign	Medina	8
99	Zalzalah	Earthquake	Makkah	8
100	'Adiyat	Chargers	Makkah	11
101	Qari'ah	Clatterer	Makkah	11
102	Takathur	Rivalry	Makkah	8
103	'Asr	Afternoon	Makkah	3
104	Humazah	Backbiter	Makkah	9
105	Fil	Elephant	Makkah	5
106	Quraysh	Quraysh	Makkah	4
107	Ma'un	Charity	Makkah	7
108	Kawthar	Abundance	Makkah	3
109	Kafirun	Unbelievers	Makkah	6
110	Nasr	Time	Medina	3
111	Masad	Perish	Makkah	5
112	Ikhlas	Sincere Religion	Makkah	4
113	Falaq	Daybreak	Makkah	5
114	Nas	Men	Makkah	6

*The article "the" that should proceed the surahs' names has been removed for the sake of brevity. The article "the" is the equivalent of the Arabic article "al," which proceeds all the original names of the surahs.

APPENDIX B

Chronology of the Qur'anic Surahs

The Qur'an was revealed over 23 years—13 years in the city of Makkah (Mecca) and 10 years in Medina. Prophet Muhammad received the first Qur'anic revelation in 610 A.D. in the city of Makkah. Eighty-eight of the 114 surahs were revealed in Makkah prior to the migration of the Prophet to Medina in 622 A.D. The Medinan surahs are, however, larger in size and constitute the bulk of the Qur'an. Out of the 30 parts (*juzu'*) that make up the Qur'an, only 11 are of Makkan origin, while the remaining 19 are Medinan.

Surahs of the Qur'an are not chronologically ordered but rather in accordance with the directive of Prophet Muhammad. According to Muslim traditions, Muhammad was given the order in which the various verses and chapters were to appear by the angel Gabriel. Gabriel reviewed the entire Qur'an with Prophet Muhammad annually and instructed him as to the proper sequence of the Qur'an.

The following table provides the chronological order of the Qur'an. The last column gives the order of surahs as they appear in the Qur'an. Notice that Surah 90, Ra'd, provides the cutting point between the Makkan and Medinan chapters. It is important to note that a surah is considered Makkan or Medinan depending on which of the cities the opening verses were revealed in. A Makkan surah could still contain verses that were revealed in Medina, and vice versa.

Chronology	Name of Surah	City of Revelation	Surah No.
1	'Alaq	Makkah	96
2	Mudaththir	Makkah	74
3	Masad	Makkah	111
4	Quraysh	Makkah	106
5	Kawthar	Makkah	108
6	Humazah	Makkah	104
7	Ma'un	Makkah	107
8	Takathur	Makkah	102
9	Fil	Makkah	105
10	Layl	Makkah	92
11	Balad	Makkah	90
12	Inshirah	Makkah	94
13	Duha	Makkah	93
14	Qadr	Makkah	97
15	Tariq	Makkah	86
16	Shams	Makkah	91
17	'Abasa	Makkah	80
18	Qalam	Makkah	68
19	A'la	Makkah	87
20	Tin	Makkah	95
21	'Asr	Makkah	103
22	Buruj	Makkah	85
23	Muzammil	Makkah	73
24	Qari'ah	Makkah	101
25	Zalzalah	Makkah	99
26	Infitar	Makkah	82
27	Takwir	Makkah	81
28	Najm	Makkah	53
29	Inshiqaq	Makkah	84
30	'Adiyat	Makkah	100
31	Nazi'at	Makkah	79
32	Mursalat	Makkah	77
33	Naba'	Makkah	78
34	Ghashiyah	Makkah	88

35	Fajr	Makkah	89
36	Qiyamah	Makkah	75
37	Mutaffifin	Makkah	83
38	Haqqah	Makkah	69
39	Dhariyat	Makkah	51
40	Tur	Makkah	52
41	Waqi'ah	Makkah	56
42	Ma'arij	Makkah	70
43	Rahman	Medina	55
44	Ikhlas	Makkah	112
45	Kafirun	Makkah	109
46	Falaq	Makkah	113
47	Nas	Makkah	114
48	Fatihah	Makkah	1
49	Qamar	Makkah	54
50	Saffat	Makkah	37
51	Nuh	Makkah	71
52	Insan	Makkah	76
53	Dukhan	Makkah	44
54	Qaf	Makkah	50
55	Taha	Makkah	20
56	Shu'ara'	Makkah	26
57	Hijr	Makkah	15
58	Maryam	Makkah	19
59	Sad	Makkah	38
60	Yasin	Makkah	36
61	Zukhruf	Makkah	43
62	Jinn	Makkah	72
63	Mulk	Makkah	67
64	Mu'minun	Makkah	23
65	Anbiya'	Makkah	21
66	Furqan	Makkah	25
67	Isra'	Makkah	17
68	Naml	Makkah	27
69	Kahf	Makkah	18

70	Sajdah	Makkah	32
71	Fussilat	Makkah	41
72	Jathiyah	Makkah	45
73	Nahl	Makkah	16
74	Rum	Makkah	30
75	Hud	Makkah	11
76	Ibrahim	Makkah	14
77	Yusuf	Makkah	12
78	Ghafir	Makkah	40
79	Qasas	Makkah	28
80	Zumar	Makkah	39
81	'Ankabut	Makkah	29
82	Luqman	Makkah	31
83	Shura	Makkah	42
84	Yunus	Makkah	10
85	Saba'	Makkah	34
86	Fatir	Makkah	35
87	A'raf	Makkah	7
88	Ahqaf	Makkah	46
89	An'am	Makkah	6
90	Ra'd	Medina	13
91	Baqarah	Medina	2
92	Bayyinah	Medina	98
93	Taghabun	Medina	64
94	Jumu'ah	Medina	62
95	Anfal	Medina	8
96	Muhammad	Medina	47
97	Al 'Imran	Medina	3
98	Saff	Medina	61
99	Hadid	Medina	57
100	Nisa'	Medina	4
101	Talaq	Medina	65
102	Hashr	Medina	59
103	Ahzab	Medina	33
104	Munafiqun	Medina	63

105	Nur	Makkah	24
106	Mujadilah	Medina	58
107	Hajj	Medina	22
108	Fath	Medina	48
109	Tahrim	Medina	66
110	Mumtahinah	Medina	60
111	Nasr	Medina	110
112	Hujurat	Medina	49
113	Tawbah	Medina	9
114	Ma'idah	Medina	5

APPENDIX C

Prophets and Revealed Books in the Qur'an

The Qur'an identifies 24 prophets by name.

No.	Qur'anic Name	Biblical Name
1	Adam	Adam
2	Al-Yasa'	Elisha
3	Ayub	Job
4	Dawud	David
5	Dhul-Kifl	Ezekiel
6	Harun	Aaron
7	Hud	Eber
8	Ibrahim	Abraham
9	Idris	Enoch
10	Ilyas	Elijah
11	'Isa	Jesus
12	Ishaq	Isaac
13	Isma'il	Ishmael
14	Lut	Lot
15	Musa	Moses
16	Nuh	Noah
17	Salih	Shaloh
18	Shu'ab	Jethro
19	Sulaiman	Solomon

20	Yahya	John
21	Ya'qub	Jacob
22	Yunus	Jonah
23	Yusuf	Joseph
24	Zakariya	Zacharias

While the Bible does not mention the name of Prophet Muhammad, the Gospel of John (14:16, 14:26, 15:26, 16:7, 20:22) refers to a "Paraclete" who will come to help the followers of Jesus (John 14:16).

The Qur'an states that Jesus did inform his followers of the coming of a messenger whose name would be "Ahmad," or "the one who is often thanked": "And remember, 'Isa bin Maryam (Jesus, son of Mary) said: O children of Israel! I am the apostle of God (sent) to you, confirming the law (which came) before me, and giving glad tidings of a messenger to come after me, whose name shall be Ahmad. But when he came to them with clear signs, they said, this is evident sorcery!" (Saff 61:6).

The word "paraclete" has been translated as the person who "counsels," "helps," or "comforts." The Qur'an calls the one who will follow Jesus and care for the people as the one who is "liked" and "appreciated."

The early church identified the Paraclete, however, as the Holy Spirit (Acts 1:5, 1:8, 2:4, 2:38), and Christians continue to use "Paraclete" as a title for God's spirit.

REVEALED BOOKS

Below are the revealed books named in the Qur'an:

Qur'anic Name	Biblical Name	Prophet
Suhuf	Scrolls	Ibrahim (Abraham)
Tawrah	Torah	Musa (Moses)
Zabur	Psalms	Dawud (David)
Injil	Gospel (Evangel)	'Isa (Jesus)
Qur'an	—	Muhammad

Interpreting and Translating the Qur'an

The Qur'an has been interpreted, and its meaning expounded, by many exegesists. Below are the most important commentaries on the Qur'an.

BOOKS OF TAFSIR (EXEGESIS)

1. *Tafsir Al-Tabari* by Ibn Jarir Al-Tabari
2. *Tafsir Al-Qurtubi* by Qurtubi
3. *Tafsir Ibn Kathir* by Ibn Kathir
4. *Tanwir Al-Miqbas* by Ibn Abbas
5. *Tafsir Al-Baghawi* by Baghawi
6. *Tafsir Al-Kabir* by Fakhr Al-Din Al-Razi
7. *Tafsir Al-Jalalayn* by Al-Mahalli and Al-Suyuti
8. *Dur Al-Manthur* by Al-Suyuti
9. *Ruh Al-Ma'ani* by Mahmud Al-Alusi
10. *Ma'ariful Qur'an* by Mufti Shafi Usmani
11. *Al-Kashshaf* by Al-Zamakhshari
12. *Fath Al-Qadir* by Muhammad Al-Shawkani

The Qur'an has also been translated into many languages, including English. Muslim scholars have always insisted that rendering the Qur'an into another language is an act of interpretation by the translator, and hence they insist that the translation is not a substitution for the Arabic original. Below are the most important translations available today in English.

ENGLISH TRANSLATIONS OF THE QUR'AN

1. Abdullah Yusuf Ali, *The Meaning of the Holy Qur'an* (Beltsville, MD: Amana Publications, 1983)

2. Arthur John Arberry, *The Koran Interpreted: A Translation* (Clearwater, FL: Touchstone, 1996)
3. Muhammad Asad, *The Message of The Qur'an* (London: The Book Foundation, 1980)
4. M.A.S. Abdel Haleem, *The Qur'an* (Oxford University Press, 2004)
5. Zohurul Hoque, *Translation and Commentary on The Holy Qur'an* (Lahore, Pakistan: Holy Qur'an Publication, 2000)
6. T.B. Irving, *Noble Qur'an: Arabic Text & English Translation* (Beltsville, MD: Amana Publications, 1991)
7. E.H. Palmer, *The Qur'an: The Sacred Books of the East* (Danbury, CT: Rutledge, 2001)
8. Marmaduke Pickthall, *The Glorious Qur'an* (New York, NY: Everyman's Library, 1993)
9. John Meadows Rodwell, *The Koran* (Blaine, WA: Phoenix Publishing, 2003)
10. M.H. Shakir, *The Qur'an* (Elmhurst, NY: Tahrike Tarsile Qur'an, 1999)

Glossary

'Ahd (covenant) an oath taken by individuals or group representatives to abide by a written or verbal agreement

Akhlaq moral values; the term is very often used in reference to individual moral traits

Alhamd or Hamd the act of praising God and recognizing his greatness

Allah the word used to refer to the Divine, the Arabic equivalent of the word "God"

Ansar (supporters) the Muslims of Medina who supported the Prophet and gave shelter to Muslim immigrants from Makkah

'Aqd (contract) a contract and/or agreement subject to legal regulation and enforcement

'Aql (reason) the rational capacity of humans

Ayah a verse of the Qur'an

Batil a Qur'anic term referring to a state of corruption and deviance

Bay'ah a declaration of allegiance to political leadership; in classical Muslim political theory, *bay'ah* is the consent of the ruled given to political authority

Companions the close associates of the Prophet

Dawlah a political state; polity

Dhimmi a covenanter; in classical Islamic jurisprudence, a non-Muslim who entered into a peace covenant with the Muslim community

Din religion

Du'a supplication in which the faithful seek God's forgiveness and support

Dulah circulation of wealth among a social group or class

Falasifa philosophers

Fiqh the term is often used in reference to the body of rules of conduct derived by Muslim jurists from the Islamic sources; the Qur'an uses the term to refer to the proper understanding of the revealed word

Fitra human nature, which in the Qur'anic conception is pure and balanced

Fu'ad human rational capacity, which the Qur'an describes as closely interconnected with human emotions

Fuqaha Muslim jurists

Ghayb the unseen, the beyond, the transcendental reality that constitutes the notion of truth

Hadith a narration by a companion of the Prophet regarding the Prophet's statements and actions; hadiths are a major source of Islamic law

Hajj (pilgrimage) an annual visit to Makkah—one of the pillars of Islam; Muslims who have the financial means are required to visit Makkah at least once in a lifetime during the 12th month of the Muslim calendar, to perform the rituals of *hajj*

Haq what is true and right, the principle upon which the natural and human orders rest

Haram attitudes and actions prohibited by divine revelation

Hikmah wisdom

Hiyal shar'iyyah legal devices or tricks introduced by late Muslim jurists to sidestep the rulings of Islamic law

Hudud (limits) the upper limits of punishment in Islamic penal code

Huquq plural of *haq* (see above)

Huquq al-'ibad legal protections of individual rights in Islamic law

Huquq Allah individual obligations toward Allah

Ibadat (rituals) acts of worship, such as prayer, fasting, and the like

Iblis Lucifer, the rebellious one, also Satan, who was from the *jinn* species and refused to comply with the divine commandment to bow down to Adam

Ijma' (consensus) a *shari'ah* ruling that receives wide support by different Muslim jurists

Ijtihad the intellectual efforts exerted by a scholar to arrive at a *shari'ah* ruling, as well as the outcome of those efforts

Ikhtiyar the process by which a ruler is selected; the concept was developed by Sunni scholars to counter the Shi'a claims that the Prophet designated his cousin Ali bin Abu Talib as his successor

Iman the state of being faithful

Israf indulging in extravagance and transgressing limits, leading to injustice, aggression, and sin

Jihad exertion of one's effort to adhere to and promote divine principles; *jihad* spans a variety of activities, including developing self-control, seeking knowledge, performing community service, and fighting to repel aggression and defend the oppressed

Jinn an intelligent species created from fire

Khalifah (caliph) the title that was historically given to the highest political office in the territories ruled by Muslims; the Qur'an uses it in reference to the moral agency of humans as they act in the capacity of being the vicegerents of God

Kufr (infidelity) the mental and practical state of rejecting divine revelation.

Luqman a wise man cited in several surahs of the Qur'an; some commentators on the Qur'an have argued that he was a prophet

Makkan the adjective form of Makkah; the birthplace of the Prophet and the holiest site in the world of Islam; also "Mecca"

Makruh reprehensible actions; a category of Islamic law

Mandub recommended actions; a category of Islamic law

Maqasid (purposes) the purpose for which a divine directive was revealed, also the purpose of actions; a category of Islamic law

Ma'ruf actions that are commonly acceptable and agreeable in society; opposite of *munkar*

Masalih public interests and common good; a category of Islamic law

Millah or Millet a religious community, also the political system implemented historically by Muslim states that recognized the moral autonomy of religious communities

Milli an adjective form of *millah* (see above)

Mithaq (pact) an agreement among groups with internal solidarity

Mu'amalat (transactions) the branch of *fiqh* that regulates trade and commercial transactions

Mubah (permissible) actions that are neither recommended or commanded; a category of Islamic law

Muhajirun the early Muslim who immigrated from Makkah to Medina to join the Ansar and form the first Muslim community

Munkar the subversive and antisocial behavior that the overwhelming majority find reprehensive

Mutakalimun Muslim theologians; the singular form is *mutakalim*

Qada' fate; divine judgment that predetermines

Qadar destiny; the impact of divine judgment, or fate, on the life of the individual

Qawamah a Qur'anic concept that connotes authority, responsibility, and protection

Qiyas (analogy) a procedure in Islamic jurisprudence that allows the jurist to extend the application of a rule to similar cases; unlike the deductive procedure used in formal logic, the expansion of the rule does not require a general premise but is done by employing particular premises

Ra'i (opinion) a conclusion reached by an individual jurist or scholar; unless it is backed by other jurist, the conclusion reflects the personal understanding of the jurist and has less weight than a conclusion that received wider support or the consensus of the scholarly community

Ridda (apostasy) the act of renouncing one's faith

Salah prayer; Muslims are required to pray five prayers every day with prescribed recitation and movements

Salam peace

Sha'air rituals; symbolic acts intended to reaffirm and strengthen faith

Shari'ah (Islamic law) the word refers to the different pronouncements and directives in Islamic revelation; it is often used in reference to the *fiqh* rulings

Shi'a the term was originally used to refer to the followers of Ali bin Abu Talib, the cousin of the Prophet, the fourth Khalifah. By the fifth Islamic century, the Shi'a took the form of an Islamic sect with distinct doctrines and rituals that set them apart from the Muslim majority, the Sunni.

Shi'i the adjective form of Shi'a; also used as noun to denote the followers of Shi'a

Shukr shukr is the gratitude one expresses for the good he receives

Shurah mutual consultation

Siyasah politics or the science of politics

Sunnah the term used to denote both the main branch of Islam and the practice of the Prophet

Surah chapter of the Qur'an; the Qur'an is divided into 114 surahs

Tafsir the scholarly interpretation of the Qur'an; the term is also used to denote the act of interpretation in general

Takfir the excommunication of a Muslim or a group of Muslims by other fellow Muslims, a practice rejected by many Muslim scholars and jurists, because it is considered to be a divine prerogative and none within the Muslim community can claim to speak on behalf of the Divine

Taqwa the state of awareness of God and one's obligation towards him, often translated as the fear of God, God-consciousness, or piety

Tawakkul placing one's trust in God

Tawhid believing in the oneness and unity of the Divine

Uhud plural of *ahd*

Ulama Muslim scholars, particularly those trained in *shari'ah* sciences

Ummah the Muslim community

Uqud plural of *aqd*

Usul roots of basic principles

Usul and fiqh the principles of Islamic jurisprudence, consisting of methodological questions and procedures

Wajib (duty) actions obligatory to Muslims; a category of Islamic jurisprudence

Wazir (minister or secretary) a public official empowered by the ruler or sultan to oversee a particular area of public policy or to act on behalf of the ruler

Zakah obligatory charity required from Muslims, which amounts to 2.5 percent on personal wealth and 10 percent on productive wealth

Zandaqah heresy

Zann (conjecture) a statement the reality of which cannot be ascertained; knowledge that is less than certain, whose truth ranges between the possible and the probable

Index

About the Author

LOUAY M. SAFI is Executive Director of ISNA Leadership Development Center (ILDC), Plainfield, Indiana. He is a fellow of the Institute for Social Policy and Understanding and serves on the steering committee of the Muslim-Christian Initiative on the Nuclear Weapons Danger. He is the author of eight books, including *Tensions and Transitions in the Muslim World* and *Peace and the Limits of War.* He has served as the Executive Director and Director of Research of the International Institute of Islamic Thought, Editor of the *Journal of Islamic Social Sciences,* and President of the Association of Muslim Social Scientists. Safi taught at Wayne State University, and he served as Visiting Professor at George Washington University and as Associate Professor of Political Science at the International Islamic University of Malaysia.